sculpted band saw boxes

Lois Keener Ventura

POPULAR WOODWORKING BOOKS
CINCINNATI, OHIO
www.popularwoodworking.com

Disclaimer

To prevent accidents, keep safety in mind while you work. Use the safety guards installed on power equipment; they are for your protection. When working on power equipment, keep fingers away from saw blades, wear safety goggles to prevent injuries from flying wood chips and sawdust, wear hearing protection and consider installing a dust vacuum to reduce the amount of airborne sawdust in your woodshop. Don't wear loose clothing, such as neckties or shirts with loose sleeves, or jewelry, such as rings, necklaces or bracelets, when working on power equipment. Tie back long hair to prevent it from getting caught in your equipment. People who are sensitive to certain chemicals should check the chemical content of any product before using it. The authors and editors who compiled this book have tried to make the contents as accurate and correct as possible. Plans, illustrations, photographs and text have been carefully checked. All instructions, plans and projects should be carefully read, studied and understood before beginning construction. Due to the variability of local conditions, construction materials, skill levels, etc., neither the author nor Popular Woodworking Books assumes any responsibility for any accidents, injuries, damages or other losses incurred resulting from the material presented in this book. Prices listed for supplies and equipment were current at the time of publication and are subject to change.

The intent of this book is to instruct the reader in the reproduction of these designs for personal use. Reproductions of these designs for profit violates copyright laws.

Metric Conversion Chart

to convert	to	multiply by
Inches	Centimeters	2.54
Centimeters	Inches	0.4
Feet	Centimeters	30.5
Centimeters	Feet	0.03
Yards	Meters	0.9
Meters	Yards	1.1

Distributed in Canada by Fraser Direct
100 Armstrong Avenue
Georgetown, Ontario L7G 5S4
Canada

Distributed in the U.K. and Europe by David & Charles
Brunel House
Newton Abbot
Devon TQ12 4PU
England
Tel: (+44) 1626 323200
Fax: (+44) 1626 323319
E-mail: postmaster@davidandcharles.co.uk

Distributed in Australia by Capricorn Link
P.O. Box 704
Windsor, NSW 2756
Australia

Visit our Web site at www.popularwoodworking.com or our consumer Web site at www.fwbookstore.com for information on more resources for woodworkers and other arts and crafts projects.

Other fine Popular Woodworking Books are available from your local bookstore or direct from the publisher.

12   11   10   09   08   5   4   3   2   1

Library of Congress Cataloging-in-Publication Data

Ventura, Lois Keener, 1959-
   Sculpted band saw boxes / by Lois Keener Ventura.
      p. cm.
   ISBN-13: 978-1-55870-829-7 (pbk. : alk. paper)
   1. Woodwork. 2. Wooden boxes. 3. Band saws. I. Title.
   TT200.V495 2008
   684'.08--dc22

                              2008003371

Acquisitions Editor: David Thiel
Senior Editor: Jim Stack
Designer: Brian Roeth
Production Coordinator: Mark Griffin
Photographers: Lois Keener Ventura, Jim Stack, David Thiel
Illustrator: Jim Stack

About the Author

Lois Keener Ventura has been woodworking most of her life. She designed, sculpted and exhibited band saw boxes and other woodworks professionally for eleven years. During that time, she earned several awards and invitations to juried art shows; collectors worldwide own her work. She also photographed and authored *Building Beautiful Boxes With Your Band Saw* (Popular Woodworking Books, 2000)

Medical issues curtailed Lois' full-time woodworking, but she still takes on occasional woodcraft challenges both in and out of the shop. Strolls with her staunch dogwood pal, Stick, and joyful visits with old and dear woody friends in their Appalachian Mountain neighborhood are a continued inspiration. Lois and her husband Peter have planted more than one hundred trees and are long-time environmental advocates. One of Lois' many favorite Native American maxims: *"Whenever you take anything from the Earth, remember to leave an offering."* (JOE COYHIS, MOHICAN)

Dedication
TO SARGE AND STICK

Acknowledgements
Much credit goes to master craftsmen and editors extraordinaire, Jim Stack and David Thiel. Without their creative genius, woodworking expertise and patience with my pickiness (well, I like to think of it as my "attention to detail"), this book would not have been possible. (Yes, those are Jim's and David's hands in many of the photos; I haven't gone on steroids!) For this book, Jim and David have realized in wood for the first time nine new box designs I haven't gotten a chance to sculpt myself.

And special thanks to: My hardy, faithful fellow mountaineers, Victoria Bell and Steve Du Pre, for their rock-like support, leather boot encouragement and tolerance to extreme conditions (particularly the winds of my verbosity); my husband, Peter, and our feline fuzzballs of joy, Pussers, Pies, Squatch and Tuggs, for their constant distraction as I attempted to concentrate on this book; Scroller David Newman, Shaper Scott Deming, Box Makers Nick Molignano and Jeff Vollmer and many other talented artisans too numerous to mention, whose wisdom and company were welcome respites at shows (you guys all know who you are); Tom Crabb (see Gallery introduction); Mum and Dad Keener and Mom and Dad Ventura, for their patience and support during those frenzied art show years; and Mum also for teaching me very early to perceive and value with all my senses the wonders, great and small, of Earth.

table of contents

introduction

the dynamics of wood

Box Sculptures: Visual Music Wood, never static, moves at speeds that defy the naked eyes of faster moving mortals: a symphony of rings, grain and colors may play right before your eyes, yet the unseen expansion and contraction of wood's microscopic fibers is revealed only when a door sticks tight one day but on another day magically opens with barely a touch.

It's no secret that wood's dynamics inspire many a woodworker. So just how does a woodworker immortalize this awesome attribute in wood? By sculpting fun, fascinating band saw boxes, of course! Functional, yet each sculpture is as fluid as the tides, as diverse as the world that rewards our senses so keenly. A box sculpture can be as simple as a solo recital or as complex as a multi-movement concerto. Music for your eyes, a sculpted box's lines flow, meander, rise and fall into carefully orchestrated parts that comprise the whole of the piece.

But best of all, band saw box sculptures encourage you to improvise. Chuck the conductor's baton: pitch that ruler! Precision is variable; freedom rules! There's no need for a shop chock full of tools, jigs, blades and bits in every size and shape. With just a few basic woodworking instruments, you'll discover your own dynamics that many other styles of woodworking don't allow you the freedom to explore.

"Hey, that's really cool! How'd you do that?" Green and seasoned woodworkers alike would stop by my display at exhibitions where they'd examine drawers and caress enticing curves with that woodworker's gleam in their eyes. It wasn't long before I realized it wouldn't be fair to hoard the joy of improvising band-saw box music all to myself. So I shared some of my patterns, tips and techniques in *Building Beautiful Boxes With Your Band Saw* (Popular Woodworking Books, 2000).

Soon, letters and emails with photos of beautiful work arrived in my mailbox and through cyber space from woodworkers now hooked on this style of box making. Duly proud woodworkers duplicated the designs in the book with im-

IN THIS PHOTO DAVID THIEL IS ON THE LEFT AND JIM STACK IS ON THE RIGHT, BUT NOT NECESSARILY POLITICALLY.

pressive accuracy, displayed awards they'd won at local craftsman's guilds, and shared their own innovations with tools they had on hand. It was so rewarding to see so many fellow woodworkers having so much fun making these boxes!

Variations on a Theme These thirty new designs in *Sculpted Band Saw Boxes* build on the *Building Beautiful Boxes* overture. A new line of functional box sculptures — what a fun, challenging way to fine-tune your contemporary organic woodworking skills!

With this second movement come variations on the theme — a couple of new voices join the box-sculpting chorus. Popular Woodworking editors and veteran woodworkers Jim Stack and David Thiel offered to sing much of the *Sculpted Band Saw Boxes* song if I provided the "sheet music" (my designs, that is — nine of which they demonstrate their interpretation of processes unique to each box). They also asked me to provide a gallery of my box sculptures and a bit of insight into where these designs and this style of woodworking came from as inspiration throughout my own box-sculpting concerto.

Jim and David use some different tools, techniques and personal variations that I've never tried (or never even thought about trying) with these designs. It's my hope that their diverse perspectives will encourage woodworkers to further experiment with this freeform, organic style of woodworking, and help to present it in a way that makes it as timeless as any classic woodworking style.

"We do not inherit the Earth from our Ancestors; we borrow it from our Children."
(Native American Proverb)

It's also my hope, through this woodworking style and theme, to ensure that coming generations will still have woodlands to inspire them, wood in which to carve their creativity and wood's glowing warmth to live alongside. May they know that we had the forethought to conserve earth's dynamic treasures for them. And may you sustain the inner dynamics that make your own visual music timeless with each band saw box you sculpt! LKV

how-to overview

by JIM STACK

Based on *Building Beautiful Boxes with Your Band Saw* by Lois Keener Ventura

Box Steps Yes, you could say building these boxes is like dancing. Your partner is that beautiful wood you've just found or have been secretly saving for the past decade and the music is the hum of your power and hand tools.

These designs range from easy to intermediate, depending mainly on the number of drawers and amount and type of carving involved. Most carving and shaping can be done quickly with coarse-through-fine sandpaper on a belt sander, oscillating drum sander and with sanding drums on a portable drill, then refined with a finishing sander and hand sanding. But, some carving on most of the designs — mainly saw kerfs — must be done with straight chisels and lots of coarse-through-fine sandpaper wrapped around dowels, flexible rubber sanding accessories if you have them, and, of course fingers. (You definitely need these, so take special care around a running band saw blade!)

Basic Tools List: Table saw; 14" band saw; $^3/_{16}$" band saw blades; wood glue; a variety of clamps; stationary belt sander; portable drill and 1" × 2" sanding drum; finishing sander; sheet sandpaper in 80, 120, 180 and 220 grits; coarse, medium and fine grit sleeves for drums and belts. Optional Tools: $^1/_4$" band saw blade; oscillating spindle sander; plunge router; router table; flocking kit.

When selecting wood, look for grain patterns that are exceptional. Burls, curls, spalting, unusual colors and yes, even cracks, splits, worm or bug holes and checks can be used to create a box that will truly be one of a kind.

When you cut a board into shorter lengths, inspect the end grains and match them to each other, such as bookmatching or run the grain in a sequential pattern. This can make your box sing a tune that no one has ever heard.

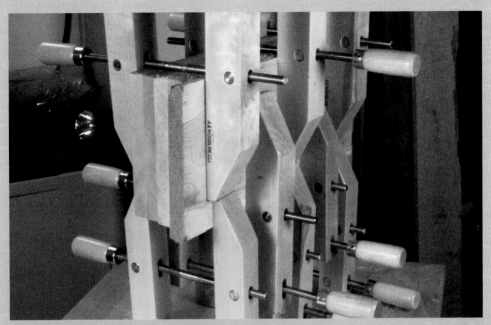

HAND SCREWS — A BOX-MAKER'S BEST FRIENDS

After you've selected your wood and chosen a nice-looking grain pattern, you'll need to glue up the sandwich. Wooden handscrews are the best choice for clamps. (You can never have enough handscrews, as shown in this photo.) They apply even pressure at all points on the glueup.

BE AWARE OF SQUARE

Flatten the bottom squarely to the back of your box blank. A jointer is obviously the easiest tool to use for this operation, but a hand plane, a disc sander or a stationary belt sander will also work.

BACK OFF FIRST

First, cut the 1/4"-thick back off the box blank.

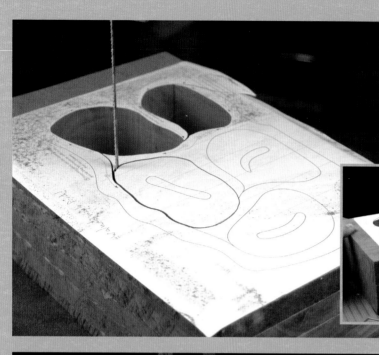

THE BOX-CUTTING JOURNEY

Make a copy of the box pattern and attach it to the front of the box blank using a spray adhesive. Start by cutting on the pattern lines. Each box has its own map of the cutting journey, so get your directions straight before starting. Cut out the drawers and sand the cutouts if necessary.

BACK BACK ON

Glue the back back on the box. My supervisor showed up to inspect my work. I passed — this time. After the glue is dry, cut out the outside box shape and sand it smooth using an ocillating spindle sander (see inset above), an ocillating sander and/or hand sanding.

DRAWER FRONT AND BACK BEFORE THE MIDDLE

The drawer fronts are $1/2$" thick for allow for more shaping room (photos 1 and 2) and the backs are $1/4$" thick (photo 3). The backs remain flat and the less you rip off means more drawer space.

10

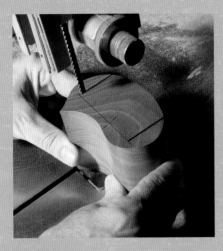  

DRAWER CAVITIES

1. Draw the cavity outline on the drawer front. If the cavity is to have square corners, make the two side-cavity defining cuts first. Note: I've raised my saw blade guard to clearly show the cutting operations. Don't do this while you are cutting! Keep the guard about 1/8" above the wood you're cutting.

2. Start at one top corner of the cavity and cut diagonally to the opposite corner, along the way cutting on about half of the bottom line of the cavity.

3. Line up on the remaining cavity piece and cut along the bottom line to create the square cavity.

BACKS BACK ON THE DRAWERS
Glue the backs back on the drawers.

THE SHAPE OF THINGS TO COME

Shaping the edges of the box can be done several different ways. The safest way (in terms of not removing too much material at a time) is to use a wood rasp. I prefer a fine-cut rasp. A coarse rasp can tear out chunks of wood at the sharp corners and delicate edges of the box.

JUST SANDING AROUND

An oscillating-spindle sander can be used to rough out areas where a fair amount of material needs to be removed. Final shaping can then be done with files and sandpaper.

ROUT ON

A router mounted in a table or handheld can be used to round over the edges of the boxes. A router is fast and unforgiving, so be sure your setup is what you want. Run test pieces to double check your setup. Note: a trimmer router is just the right size for these operations.

PULLS FOR EVERY OCCASION

Drawer pulls can add a dramatic effect to your boxes. Cutting them can be done safely on the band saw. There is no kickback — the work is held tightly to the table by the downward sweep of the blade. Trace the shapes of the pulls on the wood blank, then cut the pulls. I've raised the guard on my band saw blade for clarity. Remember to keep your guard just above the surface of the wood.

SHAPING TO SHAPE

Shaping drawer pulls can be done using the same tools used to sand the boxes, namely, an oscillating-spindle sander, a disc sander, a stationary belt sander or a hand-held belt sander clamped in a vise. Again, a power sander removes material quickly, so unless you're a safecracker, you will want to keep your fingerprints.

MORE HAND SANDING

Hand sanding is the final step.

LINE 'EM UP

After your pulls are cut out, shaped and sanded, and, when the box is ready, you can attach them to the drawer fronts. A little dab of glue will do.

DUST SAFETY — DON'T GET CHOKED UP

Cutting out boxes using your band saw, shaping with a router, belt sander, oscillating-spindle sander and hand sanding all create small particles of wood dust. These particles, when breathed

into your nose and lungs, can do damage to your body. Not today or tomorrow, but in time, the results aren't good.

The number one way to keep your nose and lungs free of wood dust is to wear a dust mask. Who is that masked man?

Here are a couple ideas that will help you collect dust at the source, namely, the machines. A shop vacuum or dust collector fitted to your machines will trap most of the wood dust.

You can build a sanding table that connects to your shop vacuum. While you're sanding parts, the down draft will direct those dust particles to go into the vacuum.

For wood dust particles with enough skill to escape the dust collector and mindlessly float around your shop, filter the air to catch them. JS

Dust Collector

Downdraft Sanding Box

Air Filter

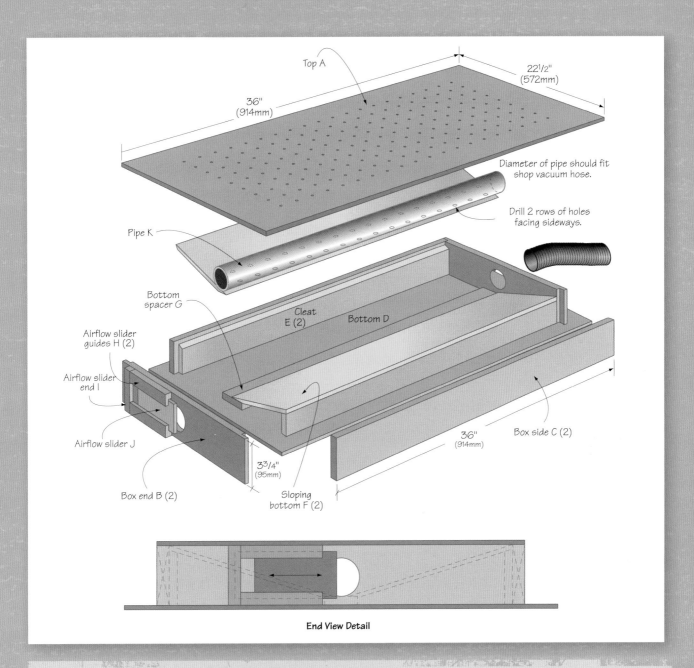

Top A

36"
(914mm)

22¹/₂"
(572mm)

Diameter of pipe should fit
shop vacuum hose.

Drill 2 rows of holes
facing sideways.

Pipe K

Bottom
spacer G

Cleat
E (2)

Bottom D

Airflow slider
guides H (2)

Airflow slider
end I

Airflow slider J

36"
(914mm)

Box side C (2)

3³/₄"
(95mm)

Box end B (2)

Sloping
bottom F (2)

End View Detail

downdraft sanding box   inches (millimeters)

REFERENCE	QUANTITY	PART	STOCK	THICKNESS	(mm)	WIDTH	(mm)	LENGTH	(mm)	COMMENTS
A	1	top	hardboard	¹/₄	(6)	22¹/₂	(572)	36	(914)	perforated
B	2	box ends	pine	³/₄	(19)	3¹/₂	(89)	22¹/₂	(572)	³/₈ × ³/₄ rabbet both ends
C	2	box sides	pine	³/₄	(19)	3¹/₂	(89)	35¹/₄	(895)	
D	1	bottom	plywood	¹/₄	(6)	26¹/₂	(673)	40	(1016)	
E	2	cleats	plywood	¹/₂	(13)	3¹/₄	(83)	34¹/₂	(876)	
F	2	sloping bottoms	plywood	¹/₄	(6)	10¹/₂	(267)	34¹/₂	(876)	16.5° bevel on one long edge and 73.5° other long edge
G	1	spacer	plywood	¹/₂	(13)	2	(51)	34¹/₂	(876)	
H	2	air flow slider guides	pine	³/₄	(19)	³/₄	(19)	5	(127)	³/₈ × ³/₈ rabbet one long edge
I	1	air flow slider end	pine	³/₄	(19)	³/₄	(19)	3¹/₂	(89)	³/₈ × ³/₈ rabbet one long edge
J	1	air flow slider	plywood	¹/₄	(6)	2³/₄	(70)	5	(127)	
K	1	pipe	PVC	2¹/₄d	(57)			35¹/₄	(895)	drill 2 rows, 16 equally-spaced ⁹/₁₆ holes

FINISH SANDING

Finish sanding isn't something you do at the end of a race. Rather, it's sanding your boxes to prep them for the application of a finish. Most woodworkers dread sanding and want it to be over as quickly as possible. However, the sanding of these band saw boxes is a crucial step. Finish sanding is what makes a good box an exceptional box. In fact, most woodworking projects that are considered high-end or fine- woodworking have been properly finish sanded. That's their secret.

How is finish sanding done and when do you know it's time to stop sanding? The top photo shows where the average woodworker will stop sanding (120- to 150-grit sandpaper). It's not bad (arrows show minute sanding scratches), it's just not quite there yet. A surface finish (lacquer, polyurethane or shellac) will fill in most minute scratches — if enough finish is applied. But those pesky scratches or tooling marks are still there, smirking and sneering at you. You wonder what went wrong. Well, nothing went wrong, you just didn't take that final step.

I recommend finish-sanding using 220-grit sandpaper (middle photo), which is readily available at your local home improvement store.

Use some mineral spirits to check the finish-sanding surface of the wood (bottom photo). This will simulate the application of finish and any fine scratches or blemishes will appear.

I talked with Lois about sanding and she said she usually finish sanded using 180-grit sandpaper on most hardwoods, 220 on softwoods using her machines and/or hand sanding. She estimates that she's made close to a thousand boxes, so I think she knows what she's doing! JS

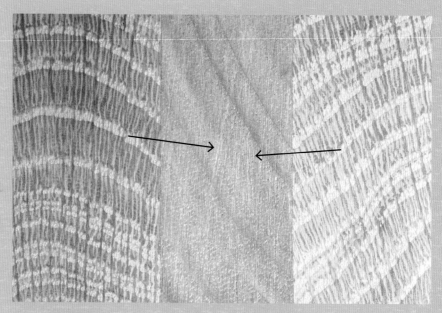

ON TO THE FINISH

After you've finish-sanded your box, it's ready to accept a finish. Now what? What is the "best" finish to use? How do you apply it?

The easiest finishes to apply are those that can be brushed on or applied with a rag. Put it on, wipe it off. Sand with 400-grit, put it on, wipe it off. Rub with No.0000 steel wool. If you like, apply some wax and wipe off. Done.

What types of finishes can you brush or apply with a rag? Shellac, polyurethane and brushing-lacquer can be applied using a brush.

You can make your own rub-on polyurethane finish by thinning the finish with 1 part paint thinner to 1 part polyurethane (see photo 1 and inset photo). If you like, add another part of boiled linseed oil for extra penetration into the wood. Other rub-on finishes are available at your local woodworking store.

Danish oil, tung oil and mineral oil can be applied with a rag or paper towels. Unless the oil has some added hardeners, oil needs to be completely rubbed off. Note: An oil finish is good for these boxes because it soaks into the wood, helping the wood stay healthy and remain more stable during seasonal changes. But, oil finishes collect dust, remain a little sticky and need maintenance coats applied every so often. I recommend top coating an oil finish using lacquer or oil-based polyurethane. You get that deep oil-finished look with the protection of a durable topcoat.

Spray finishes are another option. Use them in a well-ventilated area. Spray a light coat, let dry, sand with 320-grit sandpaper and apply another coat of finish. Sand again and do a final rub out with No.0000 steel wool.

Wax can be applied on top of any finish or no finish. Wax gives your boxes an added level of sheen and it feels good to the touch. Also, wax

will help to repel moisture (not a direct hit of water) and makes it easy to wipe away the oily fingerprints of all those who will want to touch your boxes. I prefer liquid wax because it can be spread easily using a rag. Let it dry and buff it. JS

LINING YOUR DRAWERS

As a finishing touch, you can line your drawers. These is easily done by flocking. Set up a flocking booth, using a cardboard box. Apply the glue for the flocking. See the supplier's list for flocking sources.

Use the flocking applicator to dust the inside of the drawer. Let this dry for 24 hours. After the glue has dried, shake or vacuum the excess flocking material from the drawer (I save this excess flocking to use on more drawers). The drawers are done and ready to hold your valuables.

SOME BASE BASICS

There may be occasions when you would like to display your boxes with a little more flair. Making a base to go with the box (or combination of boxes as shown above) is a great solution. The base should reflect the feel of the box so it enhances, rather than detracts from the shape and design. The carving on the bases of Lois' large projects was done with a 4" sanding disk on a heavy-duty portable 90° angle drill, and on a 6" × 48" stationary belt sander.

projects

Let's Build Some Boxes In the How-To Overview, you were shown the basic techniques needed to build band saw boxes. What follows are eight projects that each require an additional technique or two.

But the most important beginning steps from the How-To Overview to re-member before digging into any of the following projects (if not already noted in the individual project) is to square your block and rip a ¼"-thick piece off of the back of the block before cutting out the drawers. (The only exceptions to this rule are Project #5, the Contemporary Box, and its 2-drawer version on page 116.) Also remember to slice the fronts and backs off of the drawers before cut-ting out their insides. These are the 'secrets' hidden inside all of the boxes in this book.

Different finishes were used on several of the boxes to give you insights as to what finish will work on different species of wood. Experimentation with draw-ers pulls is another consideration when you're making your boxes. Pulls can add a lot to the overall look of the box. However, sometimes *not* using pulls is the best decision.

You'll also learn about an alternative band saw blade guide that is available. It can aid you in making those tight turns without binding the band saw blade and causing a bunch of smoke and noise to rise from your project.

David Thiel and Jim Stack made these projects. They are based on Lois' de-signs and her inspiration behind them, which she notes at the beginning of each project. David and Jim present fresh perspectives, new techniques, different tool options and variations on Lois' original themes — something Lois encourages so that woodworkers learn to experiment and discover their creative side.

Have fun and don't hesitate to be creative in your box-making journey!
JS and LKV

mollusk

by JIM STACK

"*There are at least 110,000 named species
and probably at least that many more still to be
discovered.*" (Raven & Johnson) Fascinating creatures such as snails, slugs, octopuses and cuttlefish
are members of this phylum. Certain mollusk species
can even craft pearls for you to store in this box, or mother of
pearl with which to embellish band saw box sculptures. Jim shows
us two species of mollusks with this project (see p. 24); you'll never run
short of models for this box. LKV

1) START BY REMOVING THE BACK

Don't even think about doing anything else until you cut away the back. Well, okay, you need to flatten the bottom of the box blank and square the back to it. But, if you don't remove the back first thing, you'll get into trouble. The back should be 1/4" thick.

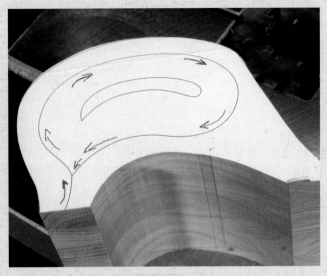

2) WHICH WAY DO I GO?

Drawing your route before you start out is a good idea. This is a basic box, so it's easy to see where to start and stop. But, boxes with multiple drawers make your journey more complicated. For this drawer, be sure to stop when you get to the saw kerf. Now, shut off your saw and let the blade come to a complete halt. Then, be sneaky and back your way out of the cut.

3) THE JOURNEY BEGINS

Once you've got clear directions, it's time to get going. Slow and steady will get you there in good shape. Let the saw blade do the cutting, don't force it. Note that the blade guide is about 1/8" above the box blank. This ensures safety and less stress on the blade, especially when making turns.

4) ON-TIME ARRIVAL

The cut is made and the journey is complete. What a trip!

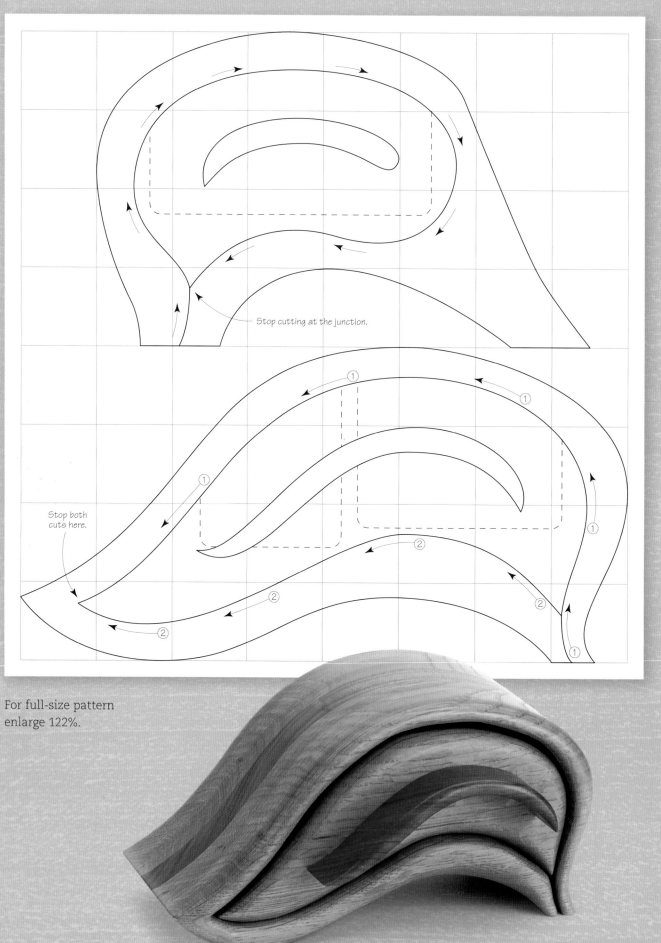

Stop cutting at the junction.

Stop both
cuts here.

For full-size pattern
enlarge 122%.

5) SANDING ROOM ONLY

I'm not telling you to go out and buy an oscillating spindle sander, but, it can become your best friend when sanding curves. You could use sandpaper wrapped around a broomstick or dowel and get good results, it just takes longer. (However, it is a great aerobic workout.) When sanding the inside of the box, don't sand any more than absolutely necessary. The idea is to smooth the saw cut a little. Removing too much material will make for a sloppy-fitting drawer. And, as everyone knows, you want your drawers to fit just right.

6) PUT THE BACK BACK ON

Now you can glue the back in place. Take the time to line up the grain patterns. Then, apply a *light* coat of glue to the back edges of the box. Clamp the back to the box and let things sit for an hour or so.

7) TRIM THE BACK

After the glue is dry, trim the back to match the box. I know what you're thinking — why did I cut out the box, cut out the drawers, glue the back on and then trim the back to the box's shape when I could have cut out the drawers, glued the back on and then cut the box to shape, saving a step? Well, I'm learning too.

which end up?

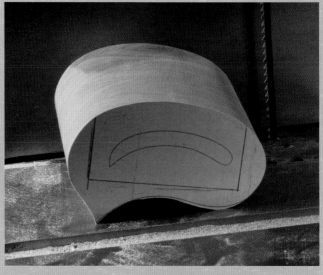

Now that you've cut out your box and its drawer, you've got a cool looking shape. That's good. But, when it comes to cutting the backs and fronts from the drawers, you need to know your best angle of attack. The left photo makes me shudder just to look at it. If you were to proceed into the saw blade, the drawer blank would be jerked out of your hands because there's no support for the bottom of the blank. If this happens, it's as if someone just put the paddles to your chest to jump start your heart. Not good. The right photo makes me happy because there's plenty of support for the blank. Proceeding into the saw blade makes it sing its happy song.

8) **CUT THE DRAWER FRONT AND BACK**
Cut the drawer front and back from the drawer blank. Failure to do this will bring the drawer police to your woodshop. The drawer back is 1/4" thick and the front is 1/2" thick.

9) DRAWER CAVITIES CHECKUP

In order for a drawer to be a drawer, it needs to have a cavity, otherwise, it's just a block of wood. Duh. With the drawer (the front and back have been cut away) in the box, draw a horizontal line to define the bottom of the cavity (I'm using the red ruler as a spacer). Then draw the vertical lines to define the sides of the cavity. The size, shape (rounded or square corners at the bottom of the cavity) and location of the cavity is up to you.

10) CREATING THE DRAWER CAVITY

Here's your chance to make a cavity and not have to go to the dentist. First, cut on the vertical lines to define the sides of the cavity. Then make a diagonal cut from either top cavity corner, catching as much of the horizontal line as possible. Finally, line up on the horizontal line and remove the waste.

11) RASPING AND FILING

This is the part that makes your box look extra special. Don't think of this as merely rounding over the edges. Think of this as shaping and sculpting the box.

12) SHAPING UP

You want the edges to flow into the curves. On both sides of this box, I've removed a little more material as I worked my way to the feet. It's subtle, but it makes a difference in how the box "sits". Look at the gallery boxes and see how Lois has left some hard edges and softened others. And notice how the edges flair in certain areas. This is the artistic part of building these boxes. I chose not use a drawer pull on this box. I drilled a hole in the back of the box. (See Project #3, page 41, step 3.)

13) THE FINISH

I brushed two thin coats of amber shellac on the box and drawer, let the shellac dry and sanded with 320-grit sandpaper. Then I applied a thicker coat of shellac, sanded it again with 320-grit. Finally, I rubbed the finish with No.0000 steel wool. A coat of wax at this point would be a good choice. I chose to take it one step further.

14) JIMMY BUFFS IT

To achieve the final high-gloss sheen on the finish of the guitars that I build, I use a buffing wheel loaded with some white polishing compound. I decided to try this technique on the box and it worked great. Now I can add a coat of wax and call it a day. Note: Since my name is Jim, I can take liberties with caption titles.

project two

stingrays

by JIM STACK

Graceful undulations propel these docile creatures along ocean currents. North of Grand Cayman Island within the confines of a protective barrier reef, stingrays are habituated to humans and will interact peacefully, accepting fishy treats from divers. This box embodies a school of rays flying in serene slow motion through calm currents. LKV

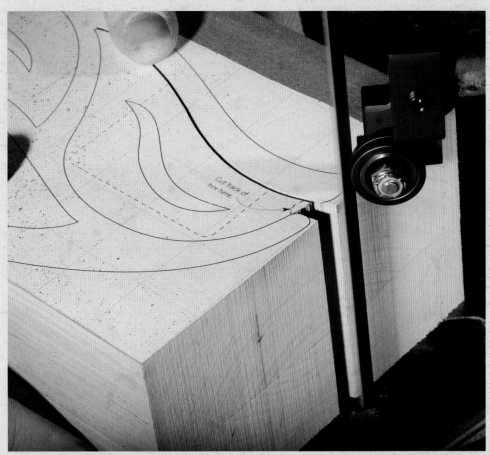

1) NOTCH AND CUT

This box has some open ends. In order to start the second cut in the right cutting plane, I cut a notch for the saw blade.

2) MAKE THE CUT

Slide the saw blade in the notch sideways and away you go. This same proceedure will need to be done on the other side of this box.

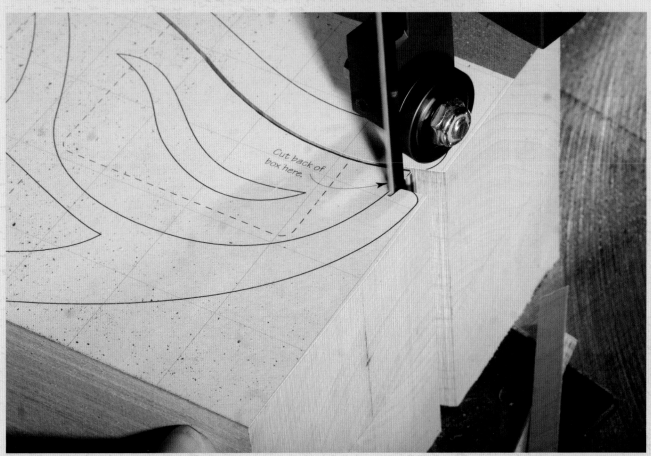

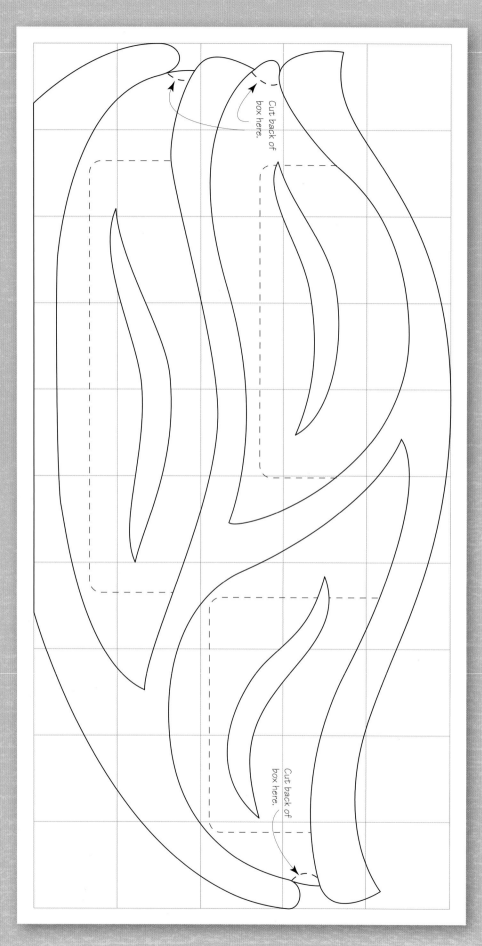

For full-size pattern
enlarge 111%.

Cut back of
box here.

Cut back of
box here.

3) MEET THE CUT

When you get to a cutting junction, stop, shut off the saw and back out.

4) SANDING INSIDE

Lightly sand (unless you want sloppy-fitting drawers) the inside of the drawer cutouts. I won't go into the ramifications of sloppy-fitting drawers.

5) SANDING YOUR DRAWERS

Lightly sand the outside of the drawers to avoid the sloppy-fitting-drawers syndrome.

6) INSPECTOR IZZY

Attach the back back on the back of the box blank. Got that? Izzy is checking the clamps, "Stack! Get over here! I think you need to tighten this one a little more."

"Looks good Jim. Now, get back to work."

7) SAND THE OUTSIDE

A disc sander is *the* tool for sanding outside curves. Light pressure is all that's needed to smooth the band saw blade marks. A heavy hand here could result in a misshapen drawer.

8) ROUGH-SHAPING

The edges of the drawers can be rough shaped using your oscillating spindle sander. Fine-tune and finish-sculpt the edges using sandpaper. Once again, remember that power tools can remove material quickly. Use a light touch and remove small amounts of material at a time. It can be heartbreaking to remove what you can't replace.

9) SHAPING THE PULLS
After cutting out the pulls, rough-shape them on your oscillating-spindle sander.

10) SANDING WITH FEELING
We had a saying in the house-finishing business, "Caulk to fit, paint to match." I've changed it a bit to fit here, "Cut to shape, sand to finish." Yeah, I know, lame. But, the idea is sound. Cutting to shape is logical. Sanding to finish means: final shaping with finesse and sanding so the look is unblemished and the feel is smooth and silky. Hmm, that still sounds lame...

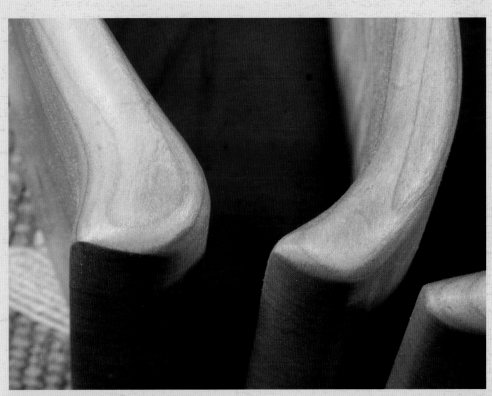

11) REVEALING
An otherwise plain-sawn face reveals its character. As the edge is shaped, the face layer seems to be coming out of the wood.

12) REAR VIEW
Here's how the back cut-outs appear when finished.

project three

andromeda

by JIM STACK

Milky Way's closest galactic neighbor. Calculations of the movements of Andromeda and our Milky Way suggest that these two big spiral galaxies may eventually collide and merge within five to ten billion years. Box sculptures last generations, but I don't think we have to worry about this one being damaged in the collision! LKV

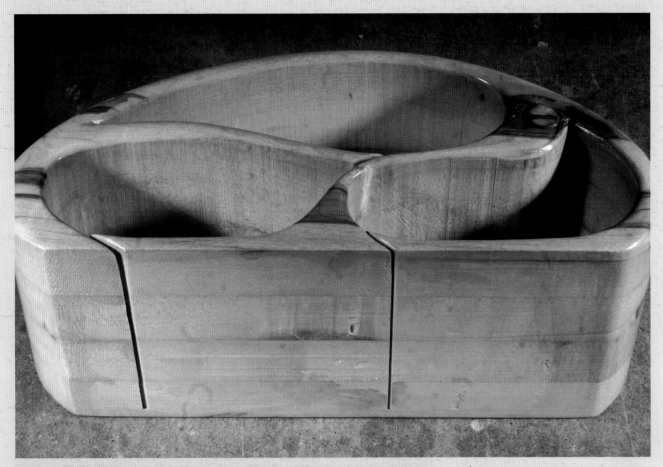

1) WHY DIDN'T YOU FOLLOW THE PATTERN?

I know you're going to notice this sooner or later: The pattern on page 40 shows one cut in the bottom. I've got two. So, what's up with that? Well, it's my box and I can make it how I want, so there. Truly though, that's the bottom line — make these boxes your own by trying something different. Really, it's okay.

2) SANDING INS AND OUTS

Generally, sanding outside curves to shape is easier than sanding inside curves to shape. That's just one of the laws of the universe. Therefore, this box is easy to sand to shape. Remove the band-saw blade marks using a sanding disc. Yes, a flat disc and make a round shape. Cool, huh?

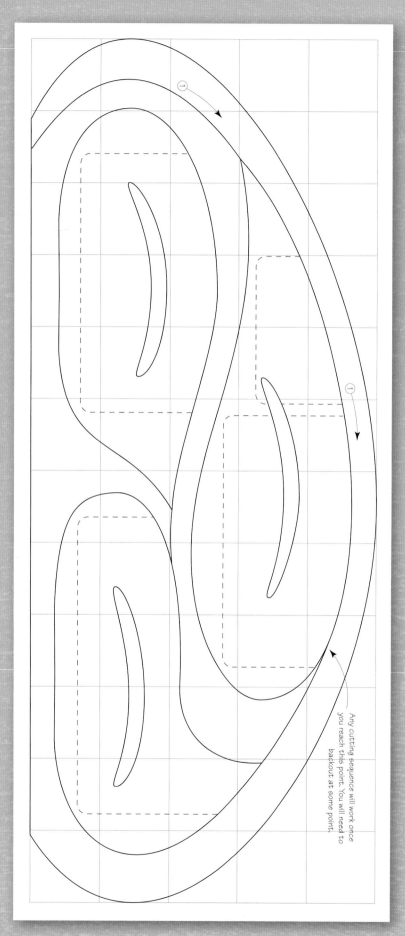

For full-size pattern
enlarge 133%.

Any cutting sequence will work once
you reach this point. You will need to
backout at some point.

3) BORING

Because I didn't want to distract from the strong grain pattern on this box's front, I chose to use no pulls. Drill a hole for each drawer in the back of the box. (The holes are used to finger-push the drawers out from the back.) Use a Forstener bit for a clean cut. Be sure to smooth the edges of the holes.

4) OUTSIDE TO FINISH

Finish sand the outside shape using an oscillating pad sander or a random-orbit sander.

41

5 ROTO-ZIPPING
The RotoZip snake attachment will make rounding over the edges of the boxes as easy as, well, zippity do da.

6 SPACING THE SPACE
This operation is fondly known as "cutting an edge". For all you skiers out there, you get it. The rest of you are asking what I'm talking about. Here's the answer — the saw kerfs should be carved and rounded over to blend with the edges of the drawer cutouts. Use a sharp knife or carving tool, then finish up with sandpaper.

7) SANDING INSIDE

Because we humans are smart, we've made a machine that bends the space-time continuum so we can sand inside curves easier than it used to be done. Remember wrapping sandpaper around a stick (not to be confused with a corn dog on a stick) and sanding while moving your wrists in an up-and-down movement? Well, those days are gone if you own or have access to an oscillating-spindle sander. Now you move the piece instead of the sandpaper.

8) FINISH, THEN FLOCK

Apply finish to the drawers before you flock them. Of course, if you're not flocking them, apply the finish and you're finished. Duh.

9) FINISH THE BACKS

Because I drilled holes in the back of the box, I need to finish-sand the backs of the drawers. It's easy to do, I just don't want to forget to do it.

10) USING THE GRAIN

This piece of wood has been sitting in my shop for almost 20 years. I finally decided to use it for this box. The key was somehow keeping the knarly holes and leached colors. I moved the pattern of the box around until both holes were in places where there would be wood. The rest of the colors fell into place.

11) WET SANDING

If you apply enough coats of lacquer or shellac (3 to 5 coats), you can wet-sand the finish before buffing it with your No.0000 steel wool. You probably won't go this far unless you're into this sort of thing. But it makes for an ultimate finish.

12) WAX ON, WAX ON

Wax is interesting. No one knows what it's made of, but it preserves peaches, strawberry jam, gives your car a showroom look, lights your way down the hall at night and helps repel fingerprints. (When I was younger, I used to chew it like gum, but that's another story.) Good stuff. Apply it to your boxes and they'll thank you around the one-hundreth time their drawers are opened.

fern leaf

by JIM STACK

There are some 12,000 species of ferns, so the variations you can make of this box should keep you busy! Lady ferns grow in abundance where I live. (They were not modest about modeling for this glamorous box.) The small drawers are designed to hold rings, and the tiny drawer pulls can represent either the dark spores that assemble in formation beneath each fingered leaflet or the gems in the rings on human fingers. LKV

1) EASIER THAN IT LOOKS

Once I got started cutting out the drawers on this box, it went smoothly and quickly. For each drawer, make either the top or bottom cut, back out and make the other cut. Do the same for each drawer and you're done quick as a bunny.

2) HOLD THE SPACE

When gluing the back in place, use a thin strip of wood to hold the space at the bottom of the box. I used white glue for this glueup because the glue will dry clear and the glue line in the maple will be invisible.

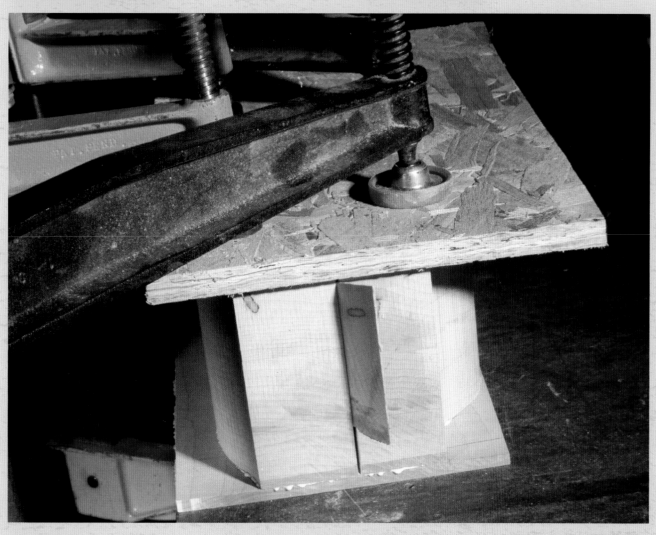

For full-size
pattern enlarge
110%.

3) LIGHTING YOUR WAY

Turn off all the lights in your shop and turn on a spotlight. Position it so it rakes across your box and creates shadows. These shadows are of great benefit when filing and sanding. The "stem" in the upper part of the photo is taking shape. The lower stem is just starting to look like its brother.

4) LIGHTING YOUR WAY

No, this isn't the slalom at Sunday River. It's another lights-out photo showing how the spotlight will reveal every filing and sanding mark. This can be good or bad, depending on how much work you want to do to reach that super-smooth surface.

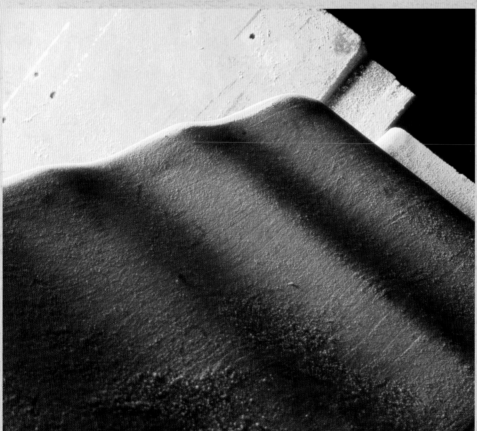

5) A LITTLE HERE, A LITTLE MORE THERE

Most of these boxes have curved lines that terminate at a point. The shaping on the edges of these curves should flow from the point or to the point, depending on how you look at it. Anyway, starting at the point, remove a little material and gradually remove more material as you move to the center of arc or curve. This gives a natural flow to the shaping.

6) BLENDING

Roundover the edges to smooth things out and blend the curves from point to point. As you do this, constantly check your progress. Don't remove too much material at the points. If you do, the flow will be disrupted and the edges will look like they've simply been rounded over by a router bit.

7) NOOKS AND CRANNIES

One thing to know about making these boxes — if you don't enjoy sanding, you might want to start woodturning or cabinet-making. However, I find this sanding relaxing. While you're picking yourself up off the floor from laughing so hard, let me say that sanding on these boxes is part of the shaping process and is essential if you want boxes that are more than just, well, boxes. Even a non-wood-worker will notice your fine sanding job if you take the time to do it.

8) LEAVES

I thought it would be interesting to apply some green paint to the drawer fronts. First, I applied a light coat of finish to seal the wood. Then, when I applied a thin coat of the latex house paint straight from the can, the paint didn't soak into the wood and have a blotchy look.

9) DETAILS

If you decide to paint the drawer fronts, apply the paint around the edges of the front and stop at the glue line where the front joins with the drawer box.

10) TO THE FINAL FINISH

First, I applied a coat of amber shellac to the box. This sealed the wood and added some depth to the color of the light maple. Then I used spraying lacquer for the topcoat. 2 or 3 coats of lacquer is fine. Remember to sand between each coat using 320-grit sandpaper. If not, you'll have a bumpy, rough finish. Yech!

11) BLENDING THE PULLS

Pulls add a lot to the gracefullness of these boxes. After you cut them out, roundover the edges and sand them, take the time to place them on the drawer front so they flow with the curve of the front. If you use the patterns, this should be an easy task.

12) THE RUB OUT

After the lacquer has cured for 2 or 3 days, sand it with 320-grit sandpaper and polish it using No.0000 steel wool. Use your task light to help you see that the sheen is even over the entire box. Then, apply a coat of wax.

contemporary

by DAVID THIEL

This is a simple-to-make box, but with a little pizzazz. No need to rip a slice off the sides of this piece before cutting out the drawers. You'd be amazed at what that gentle curve cut into those side pieces can do to make the wood grain dance! LKV

1) A CUBE

This project looks deceptively easy because of the straight lines. Not true. First you need to start with a cube. If it's not square, the sides/legs will be angled when glued in place. It's not all that easy to square a 4" cube. I started with the face/drawer front as a reference surface, then used my miter saw to trim off the roughest of the sides.

2) A TOUCH AT A TIME

I used my belt/disc sander to flatten the sawn sides. My miter saw ended up leaving a little material along one side (not a deep enough cut).

3) KEEP IT FLAT

Removing the extra material was quick, but you need to make sure that you don't lean the block too much, or you end up rounding parts that should be flat.

Pattern shown full size.

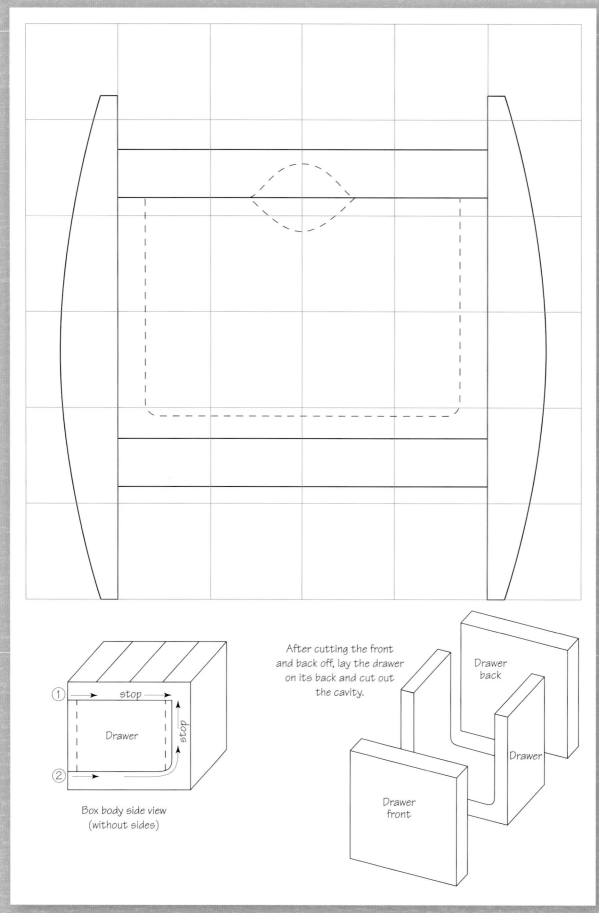

After cutting the front and back off, lay the drawer on its back and cut out the cavity.

Drawer back

Drawer

Drawer front

① stop

Drawer

stop

②

Box body side view (without sides)

56

4) NICE AND SLOW

Once you have a "flat" surface, take your time and slowly sand to a smooth finish on that face. Working with figured maple for this piece also caused me to take my time. Maple burns quickly and then it's even harder to sand the burn marks out.

5) VOILA!

With a little patience and a deft touch, the sides start to flatten and the grain begins to show its lustre.

6) SQUARE

I should have mentioned that there's more to this cube than getting the surfaces flat. They also need to be square to one another. An engineers' square will give you a quick look at how you're doing.

7) ALMOST THERE

It's much easier to mark the out-of-square surfaces and work to that line, than to sand, check and sand. Will it be a perfect cube? Probably not, but as long as the face and two sides are square, it'll work.

8) NOW THE DRAWER

As mentioned, this box doesn't require the sides to be cut from the box — they're already missing. So all you have to do is cut the drawer out of the box. This also gives you the opportunity to leave the top, bottom and back of the box intact. Mark the interior on the box, and don't forget your corner curves to help the blade work easier.

9) START AT THE TOP

While I've drawn two "round" corners, my first cut starts at the top of the box and is a straight cut to the back wall.

10) STOP AND BACK OUT

When you come to the end of the first cut. Stop the saw and back the blade out of the cut. The next cut will be a continuous cut, ending at the square corner. Note that I've marked arrows on the box to keep me spatially aware.

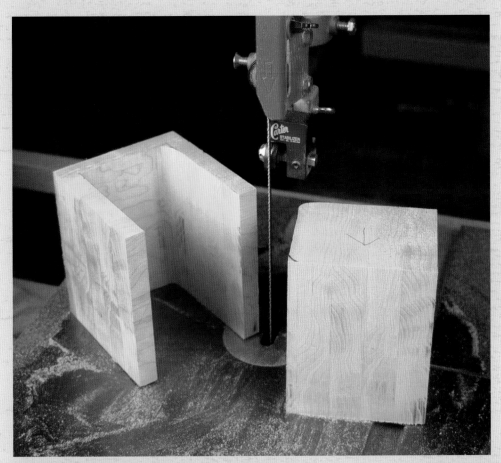

11) JUST FOR U

As you make the second cut, keep things as straight as possible (except for the corner) to give the drawer a "cube" look that will mimic the box. If you wander during the cut, you'll have to sand too much on the drawer and will lose a nice fit. With the drawer cut away from the box, you start to get a sense of the size and shape of things. Before you start to cut the drawer itself, mark the faces so you'll know how to put things back together.

12) FRONT AND BACK

Now we're back on familiar territory. Cut the ¹/₂" front and ¹/₄" back from the drawer box using the fence on your band saw to guide the cut. I made both cuts with the top of the drawer down on the bandsaw table. That way the rounded corner at the back of the box wasn't used as a reference against the fence or table.

13) IN THE DRAWER

The next step is to cut away the interior of the drawer. I'm a glutton for entertainment, so I decided this drawer needed a secret compartment under the bottom. It was simple to draw out the space (and the false bottom) on the drawer blank, then head for the saw.

14) TWO STORY

With the cutting done, you can see how the secret bottom will work. Some judicious sanding of the bottom, and where it fits against the box, will make a nice fit. If you're flocking the interior (as I was) you actually want to leave things a little sloppy on the fit to allow for the flocking.

15) LIKE MAGIC

Building secret compartments into your boxes is actually pretty easy. Once you get comfortable with the bandsawn box concept in general, it's simple to personalize. The false bottom on this drawer will simply knock out with a tap, but other secret compartments can use magnets, springs and more. Have fun!

16) A DRAWER ONCE AGAIN

A couple of light-duty clamps put things back where they belong. A little sanding on the interior (and fitting the false bottom) prior to gluing things back in place will save some frustration down the road.

17) WINGS

Contemporary this design certainly is. But, as a Star Wars fan, I couldn't help call it the TIE Fighter Box. So the legs became the wings in my mind. To get the sweeping shape on the wings, I cut apart the pattern copied from the book, then transferred that shape to a sturdier piece of cardboard. I then used that template to transfer the shape to both sides of each wing. This helps you make sure of symmetry while sanding. Note that I added a mark to the template to indicate the top edge of each wing.

18) SHAPING THE SIDES

For this cut I switched back to my ¹/₂" blade. The cut is more of a bent straight line and the thicker blade leaves a cleaner, straighter surface. I also want to include a caution here. As you guide this tall, thin piece through the blade, pull the piece with one hand on the outfeed side of the blade, guide (lightly) with your other hand. As you reach the center of the cut, the tendancy is for the blade to pop out of the side. If you're pushing with your "back" hand, it's possible to slip toward the blade. Be careful. Pull, don't push. Alternatively, you could attach the sides to the box, then cut and sand the sides to shape.

19) ROCKING THE WING

With the sides cut it's back to the sander. I again used the belt on my belt/disc sander. By applying light but consistent pressure at the center of the piece, I used a rocking motion, starting primarily at the center.

20) ROCKIN' SIDE

As you continue to rock on the sander, check your progress routinely. Those marks on both sides/ends of the wings will now help you sand to a consistent shape top to bottom and side to side. Watch your fingers as you get close to the ends of the sides.

21) OFFSET

After giving all the pieces a good sanding, you're ready to glue the sides to the box. This is made easier by using blocks, sized to the necessary offset, under the back of the box. I also used sized blocks to help with the offset at the top of the box. Fussing with a ruler while glue is drying makes for a messy box.

22) CUSTOM PULL

Custom woodworking is all about customizing. While Lois used a finger hole on her design, I decide to add a pull. I used one of the falloff pieces from the sides to create a simple walnut pull. I notched the drawer front to fit the pull and glued it in place.

23) FIT THE DRAWER

Because the drawer is exactly the same width as the box, it will need to be reduced in width to fit in the hole. Take your time and keep checking the fit to keep the spaces as even as possible. I still need a little off the top right for a nice fit.

project six

firewater

by DAVID THIEL

According to many ancient cultures, four elements create our world: Earth, Air, Fire and Water. This box sculpture represents the four elements concept, with windblown flames encased in a wave rising from the Earth's watery depths. LKV

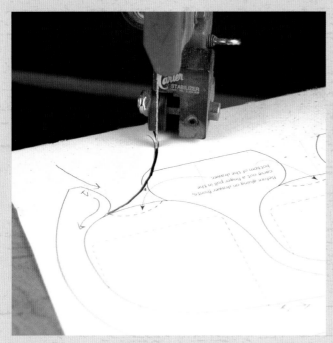

1) FIRST CUT

The design of this box utilizes finger pulls under the drawers. To access the pulls, a chunk of the box is cut away at the bottom of each drawer to let a finger in. With the back of the box cut free from the block, I start into each finger gap from one side.

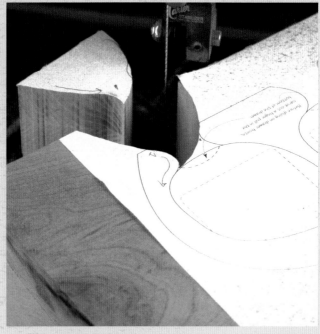

2) REMOVING THE CHUNK

While the first cut didn't follow along the edge of the box design, the second cut does, shaping along the edge of what will be the far right leg. When the two cuts connect, the chunk of wood is easily removed. I didn't complete the first "finger" area because the subsequent cuts will come back around to complete it later.

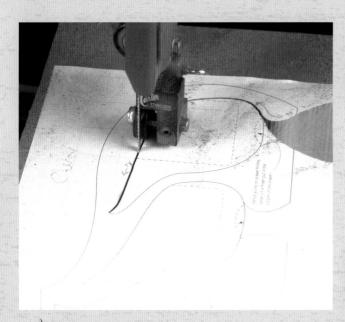

3) SWEEPING CURVE

Continuing the cut up around the far right "flame" takes a steady hand and a smooth continuation of motion. Short cuts are easier to hide a rough cut, but the long fluid sections need patience.

4) BACK TO THE TOP

To complete the first flame, it's back to the bottom and then up to meet the third cut. Your first drawer is ready to remove. Repeat these steps for the rest of the drawers.

For full-size pattern
enlarge 111%.

Before gluing on drawer fronts,
carve out a finger pull in the
bottom of the drawer.

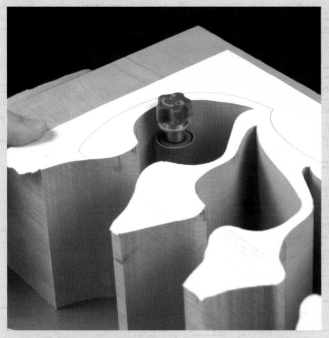

5) INNER SMOOTHING

I'm glad I had the advantage of a spindle sander for this box. Because of the rough lumber I had, the box ended up being almost 5"-deep. The spindle sander made reaching into the box cavities much easier.

6) FLIP AND SAND

Of course, 5" was still too much for the spindle sander drum, so, to reach the full depth, I ended up flipping the box over and sanding with the front side down. It would have been very difficult to sand this box with the back in place.

7) ADJUST THE FLAME

To more easily cut away the drawer interiors, I found it easiest to transfer the interior wall locations to the sides of the box before removing the front and back. I used a square to transfer the marks from the pattern on the front of the drawers.

8) CUT AND MARK AGAIN

After removing the front from the drawer, the lines made in step seven were transferred to the front of the drawer (minus the front). I first connected the two marks for the bottom of the drawer and then used that line to square up the lines for the drawer sides. Head back to the saw!

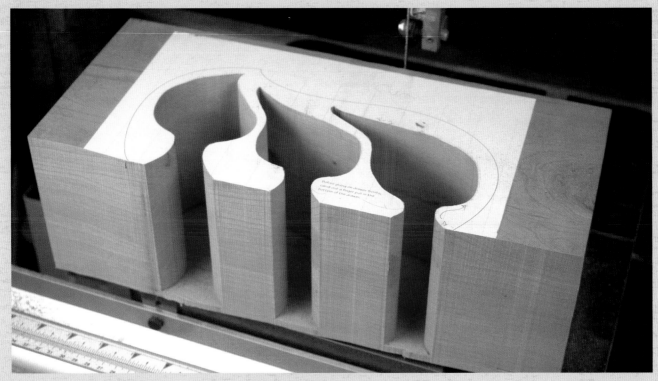

9) BACK TO THE BACK

Glue the back of the box back in place. Make sure you get adequate pressure on the center and bottom of the two inner legs. Use the drying time to cut out the interiors of the drawers. Then when the glue is dry on the box, use your clamps to glue the individual drawers back together.

10) NOTCHING THE BACK

Because we cut the back off before cutting out the drawers, we weren't able to remove the "notch" at the bottom of the back. This is a simple step with just a couple of quick moves on the saw. First define one side of the notch.

11) ...SIDE TWO

Then define the second side of the notch. There isn't any correct height to stop the notch, but essentially you can eyeball the point where the drawer starts and you want to stay below that point. A $3/4$"-diameter sanding drum can also be used to remove this material.

12) TRIM AWAY

It's very easy to discount the look of the last cut you'll make to remove the notch, but remember that this notch will be visible from the back of the box. More on that in a minute. Once the first notch is free, repeat the process for the next two notches.

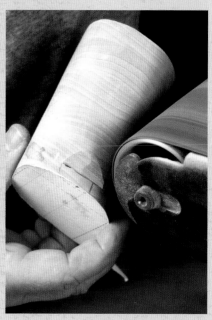

13) FINGER PULLS

Lois (being more clever than I) wisely recommends that the notch for the finger pull be carved in the bottom of the drawer box before gluing the front back on. Well, I didn't, so I needed to come up with a way to do it after the fact. And, being a bit lazy, I thought a power tool made more sense. I took a look at my belt/disc sander and realized by changing the belt tracking, I could move the sanding belt to the edge of the roller and use it as a cutting edge. I marked the pull location on the bottom of the drawer, then aligned the roller edge just behind the drawer front. You'll need to finesse the final look with sandpaper, but it works, and it's quick!

a tight-turn guide for your saw

When we started working on this book, we knew there would be a few tricky moments during the cutting that would be considered more challenging than most band saw work. Thinking along those lines, we were at a woodworking show and saw the classic "make-a-reindeer-in-two-minutes" sales pitch. When we stopped to enjoy the show, we did a double-take on the band saw guides. They were using a new guide from Carter (carterproducts.com). The Stabilizer guide supports the rear of the blade, just capturing the back edge in a notch in the replacement thrust bearing. There are no side guides on the top guide assembly. The bottom guide? Pushed out of the way entirely. We found this guide worked well in many of the tight turns, allowing a flexibility not found with standard guides. But, when it comes to larger blades, we still think the side support is important to making a straight cut. DT

14) RANDOM SANDING

The Firewater design requires a little extra sanding. Though the bottom of the box is least seen, the areas between the legs need to be sanded smooth also. A random-orbit sander did much of the work, but hand sanding was required to finish up.

15) DON'T SKIP THE BACK

Remember the notched back? It's still seen, so a little detail and carving work on the back blended the look. I found the rotary tool good for the rough shaping.

16) CREATIVE OPPORTUNITY

Depending on your mood you can simply round out the notched back, or you could add a bit of carving. I opted for gentle swells. Only the middle is near completion in this shot. Two to go.

17) FLOCKING

Flocking isn't a terribly difficult process, but tidiness will make it easier. After a top coat finish has been applied (lacquer or wax), a paint-like base adhesive is applied to the inside of the drawers. The adhesive will wipe off of finished surfaces, keeping things neat.

18) FLOCK TWO

The flocking itself is then liberally applied to the drawer. When the "paint" doesn't appear wet under the flocking, you've added enough. Leave it alone to dry overnight, then knock out the extra flocking and save it for the next project.

project seven

rock box

by DAVID THIEL

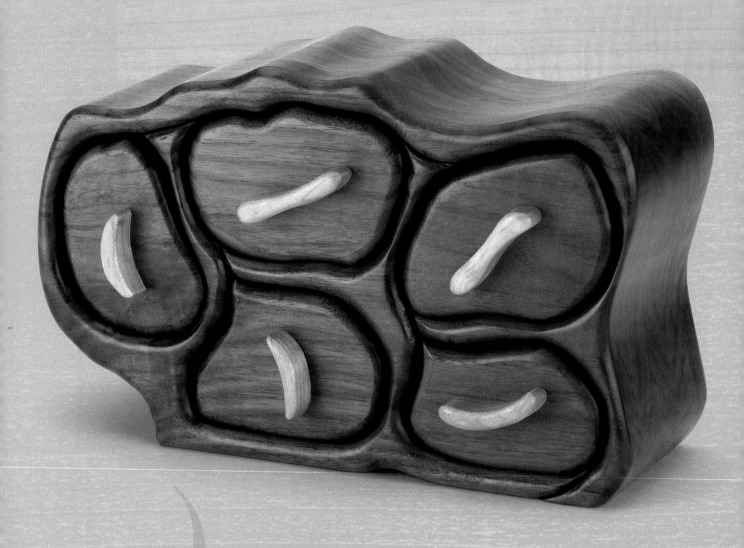

This double entendre box can be seen as a boulder encasing
your big diamonds or simply a holder for a collection of your
favorite found "lucky stones." The drawer pulls can represent
all those one-of-a-kind pebbles you find awash on the shores
and in the shallows of a rushing mountain stream. The box body
itself is modeled after the big boulders mid-stream that offer themselves up as relaxing retreats for weary woodworkers. LKV

1) IN AND OUT

This design requires you to back the blade through an existing cut in a number of places, but if you follow the pattern logically, you'll reduce those moments. The first cut wraps around the right side of the lower right drawer, comes across the bottom of the upper right drawer and then circles all the way around.

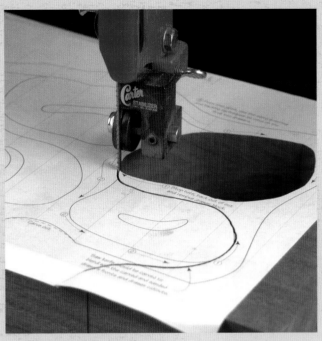

2) BACK ROUND THE STUMP

When you've completed the first cut, pop out the top right drawer, then simply reverse the travel direction and head down to the left-hand side of the lower right drawer.

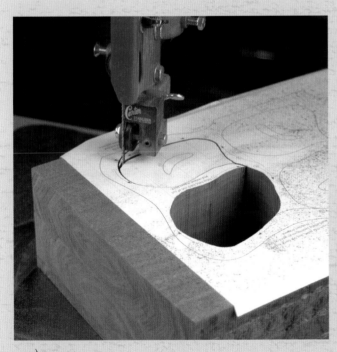

3) DRAWER TWO

When you round that drawer, pop it out as well. No blade backing required!

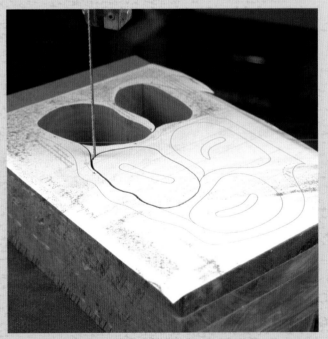

4) AND THEN.....

I think you get the idea. Swing to the middle top drawer and keep circling till all the drawers are free from the box.

For full-size pattern enlarge 111%.

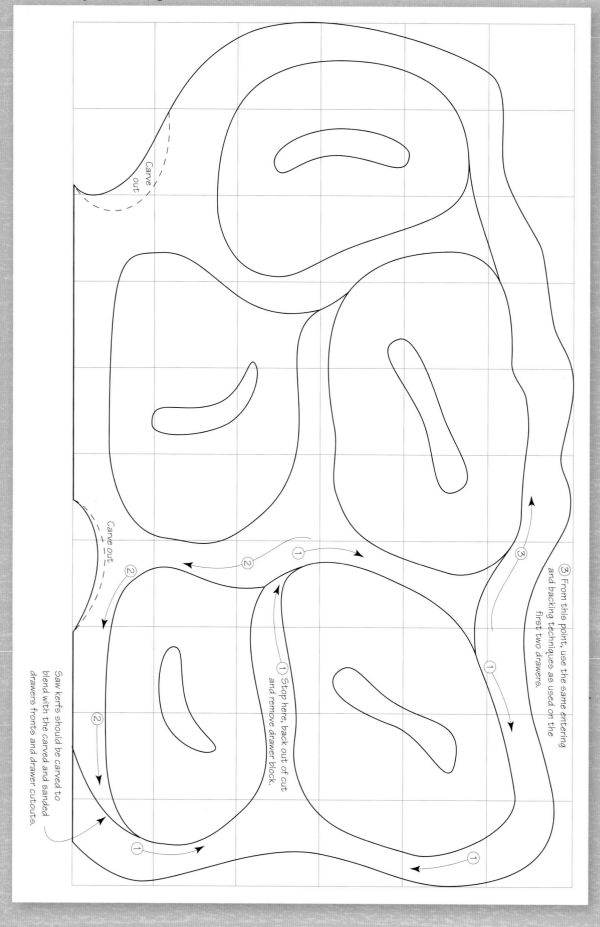

Carve out

Carve out

③ From this point, use the same entering and backing techniques as used on the first two drawers.

① Stop here, back out of cut and remove drawer block.

Saw kerfs should be carved to blend with the carved and sanded drawers fronts and drawer cutouts.

5) WHACK-A-MOLE

Okay, not really, but it looks that way. My oscillating spindle sander (popping in and out of the holes) does a nice job of cleaning up the bandsaw marks on the inside of the drawer openings. By the way, this doesn't work so well if you've already glued the back on — save that for later.

6) DRAWERS

Before you get excited and start cutting out the middle of the drawers, set your fence first for 1/2" and cut all the drawer fronts free of the boxes. Reset for 1/4" and remove the backs. Then you're ready for step one, shown above.

7) WATCH THAT CURVE!

As you move into the interior cuts on the drawers, it's up to you whether you leave a curved or squared bottom. My opinion, it's an easier turn curved, easier to sand and also leaves a more stable corner to support the drawer sides.

8) ...AND THEN

Make your left turn and head for the other corner. Nice and steady. Let the blade cut and just move smoothly. This helps a lot when you go to sand the interior of the drawers. If you don't feel like sanding, the good news is flocking hides a variety of shortcuts, and makes the drawer look nicer.

9) ...AND THEN

There, finally free. Now all you have to do is the same thing for the other four drawers.

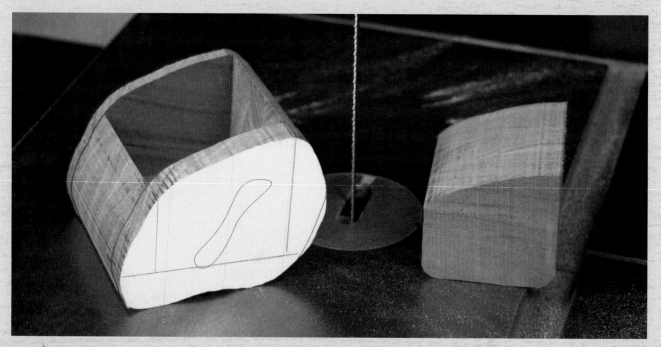

10) AND FINALLY, IT'S A BOX

In this photo, the front, back and drawer center are simply sitting together. I need to do a little interior sanding before gluing. I can't help looking at the center piece removed from the drawer and wonder what I can make with it. A box inside a drawer? You could...

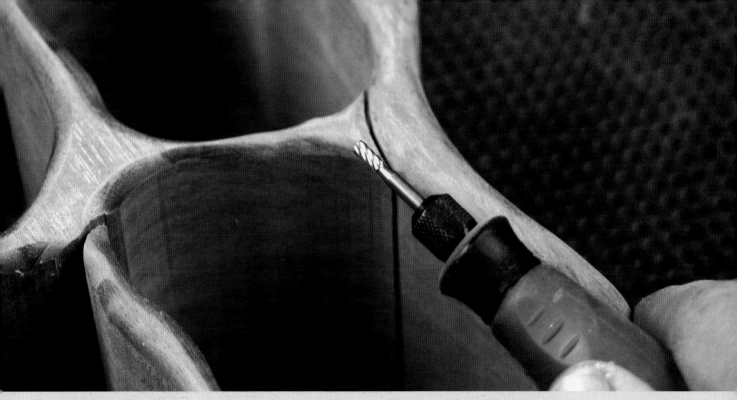

11) BACK TO THE BOX

One of the trickiest parts of detailing the box is blending the blade kerfs into the design of the box. It takes a steady hand, a good eye and the right tool. One tool that I used is a RotoZip rotary tool with an abrasive tip. This makes things move quickly — sometimes too quickly. So I also uses a set of small rasps for the final shaping.

12) HANDLES

The handles for this box are straight from Lois' design, though I did change the depth of the handles from $3/4$" to $1/2$". They just seemed a better fit. Sanding the little suckers was a little more work. I started with the outside curves on my disc sander.

13) SAVE THE FINGERS

For the inside and outside surfaces of the handles, I used the rounded end of my belt/disc sander. To keep the fingers (and fingerprints) intact, I gently grasped each handle with a pair of vice-grips. Much easier on the stomach.

project eight

twister

by DAVID THIEL

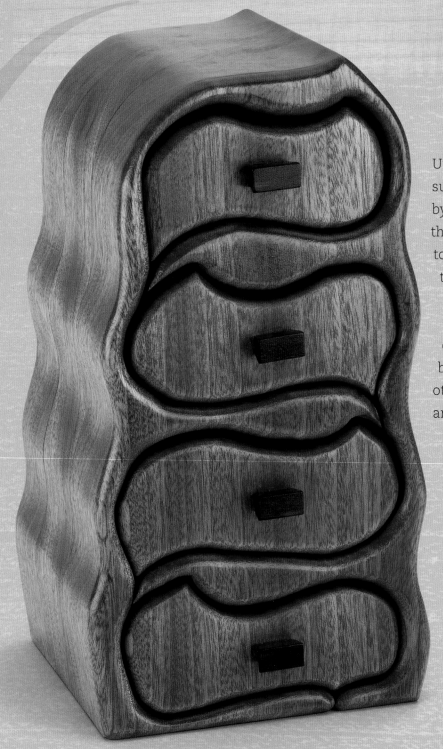

Unlike deadly debris sucked up and hurled by whirlwind monsters that swallow small towns in the heart of the U.S., the "debris" gently collected in the velvety insides of these Twisters can be gold, diamonds or other precious metals and gems. LKV

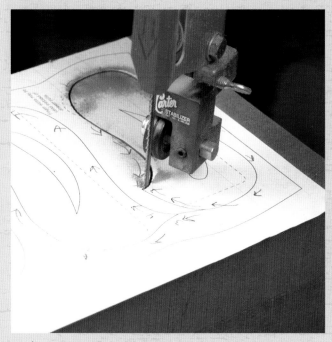
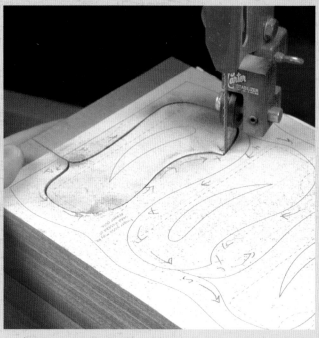

1) IN AND OUT

This box is a great-looking design, but it does require you to back the blade out of the pattern a number of times. This is cause by the peaks on the drawers. If there's a sharp peak, you can't turn sharply enough to create the point. The look is worth the effort, but be aware. The first cut starts at the bottom of the box and undulates up to the peak of the lower drawer.

2) THE OTHER SIDE

When I'd completed the cut in step one, there was enough innner tension in the wood to close the open-ing gap, making it very difficult to back the blade out. I eventually tapped a wooden wedge into the gap to make enough room to back the blade out.

3) FREE

When the second cut is complete, the drawer will be free of the box.
Stop the saw and lift the box slightly to make sure the drawer is loose.

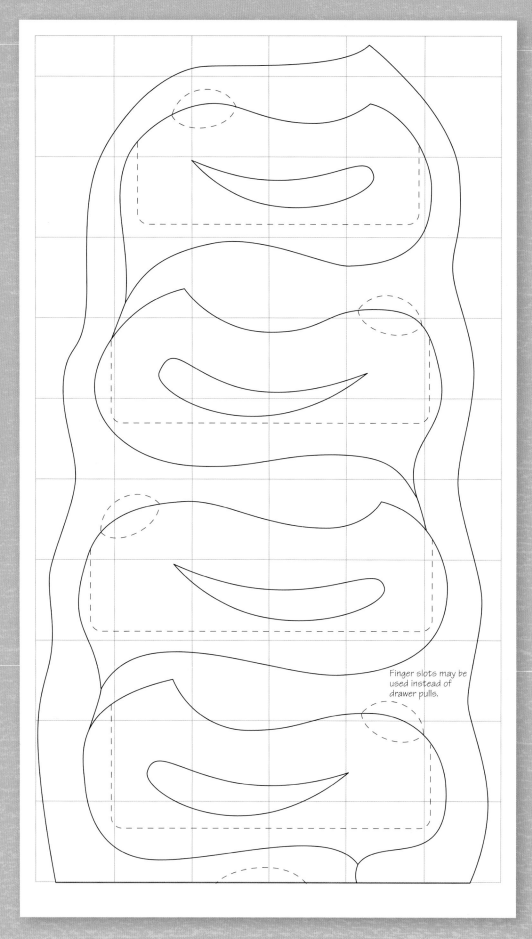

For full-size pattern
enlarge 119%.

Finger slots may be
used instead of
drawer pulls.

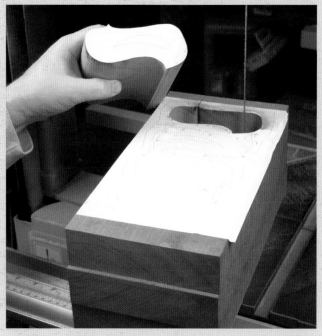

4) POP AND DROP

With the machine off, raise the guide bar and lift the box above the drawer.

5) ONE DOWN

There's no need to back the blade out this time, just let the box settle back onto the band saw table. The drawer is free and you're set up to make the next cut.

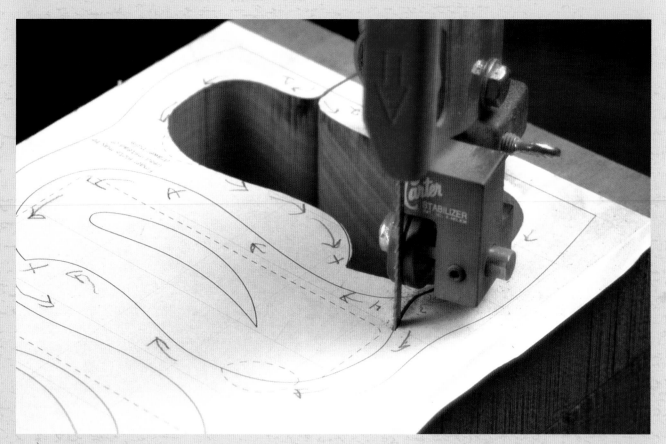

6) ROUND TWO

Start into the second drawer from the rounded left edge of the first box. Make this as smooth a transition as you can. It'll pay off in the look of the piece.

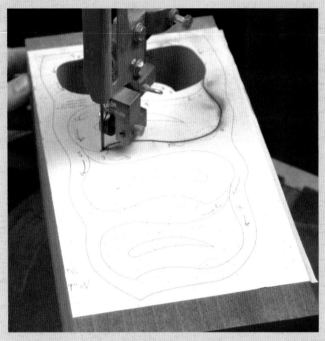

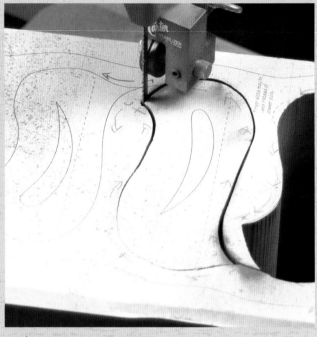

7) POINT TO THE LEFT
The rest of the box is a series of turns along one side of the box, ending in the top point.

8) POINT TO THE RIGHT
Then you back out of that cut, re-enter the cut and swing around to the other side to finish at the point again.

9) SMOOTH CURVES
With the drawers separated from the box, it's time to move to the spindle sander. These openings are a nice size to accomodate a spindle drum of a larger diameter, making it an easier sanding operation.

10) GOOD CLAMPS

Wooden hand screws are often seen as archaic and interesting, but not often used. Part of the problem, I believe, is that they take some getting used to for the perfect adjustment. It's worth the effort. These clamps are perfect for working with band saw boxes. The wide, long and flat faces allow even pressure across a number of awkward locations. As seen here, the clamps comfortably reach across each of the drawer dividers to make sure the box is strong and tight.

11) FRONT ...

While the glue on the box dries, head back to the band saw to work on the drawers. Set the fence for a ½" spacing and cut each of the fronts from the drawers.

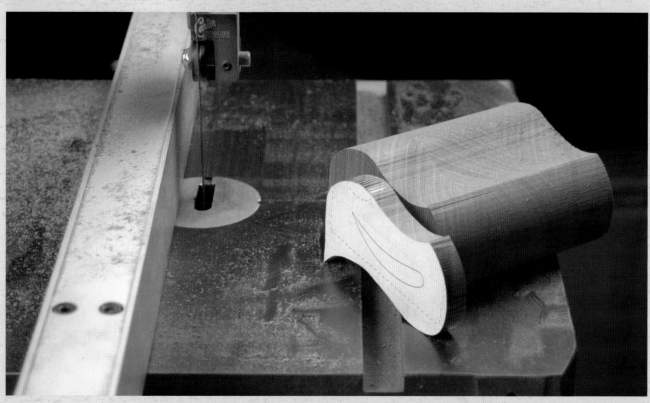

12) ... AND BACK

Reset the fence for 1/4" and repeat the process removing the backs of all four drawers. Check twice before you make the cut to ensure you're actually cutting off the back and not the front. Easy mistake.

13) OTHER CLAMPS

The other perfect clamp for band saw boxes is the one-handed, fast-adjust clamp. It only takes a little pressure to hold the drawers together, but the real benefit is in the one-hand operation. You need the other hand to adjust the pieces so they're aligned properly. Otherwise you add a lot of sanding and end up with a misshapen drawer. Oh, and the wide, soft pads on the clamps are pretty useful, too!

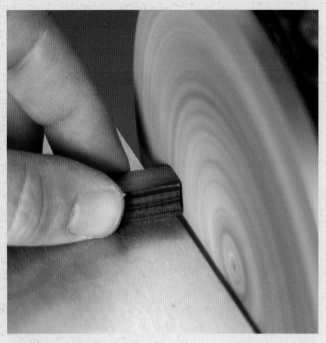

14) HANDLES

I opted for a different handle than Lois had drawn, feeling that the grain of the mahogany was so attractive that I didn't want to hide it with a larger handle. I was looking around the shop and found a left-over strip of ebony and decided that would do nicely. I first cut the handles to size ($\frac{3}{8}$" × $\frac{3}{8}$" × $\frac{3}{4}$").

15) TRAPEZOID

Rectangle didn't work for the look, so I decided to add a trapezoidal shape to the handles. This also makes them better handles, so two good reasons to get the fingers close to the sanding disc.

16) PULL!

For the longer side of the handles, I moved to the belt sander. Do be cautious here, because it doesn't take much to launch the handle across the room. It makes sense to make an extra handle or two, just in case.

17) WORTH THE TIME AND EFFORT

I think the finished look of the handles are worth the few minutes of tension. Hope you agree.

design and inspiration

by LOIS KEENER VENTURA

Shapes Rule! I used to joke that as starving artists my husband and I could only afford one ruler in the workshop. Whoever got to the workshop first got the ruler. And since I chose to savor my slice of dry bread and turbid water for breakfast, and Peter swallowed his in one gulp, well, you know who ruled that ruler! (Hint: It wasn't me.)

And that was how I started sculpting band saw boxes.

Truth is, we did have two rulers, and I always got a late start after eating twice as much granola as Peter did, then hiking through the woods near home for inspiration and the day's few minutes of sawdust-free air. And I'm sure I habitually misplaced that second ruler because I had nightmares about those multitudes of Lilliputian sixteenth-inch lines tying me to the woodshop floor forever, where I'd never be able to explore the world of woodworking beyond the constraints of a ruler.

But sharp early exploration memories quickly cut the bonds of my imaginary limitations. Playing among those memories: the vision of my grandparents' log house they hand-built from ash trees on their seven wooded acres. A wealth of warm wood pervaded that house, inside and out. Sweet applewood smoke all winter and aromatic live pine year round tantalized noses. Visual goodies abounded too. A table intricately patterned in parquetry by my great grand-father's hands adorned the smaller of two bedrooms. My grandfather crafted indoor and outdoor furniture pieces, rustic wall ornaments and walking sticks out of cherry, walnut, pine, hickory and oak scavenged from the property. The two-acre spruce forest they planted enchanted Easter Egg-hunting, tree-climb-ing grandkids for years. A woody wonderland indeed!

I never looked at old dead branches the same after Dad and PopPop shaped them into loggy picture frames or gnarled, knotty wall sconces. And thanks to Mum especially, I learned very early that the simplest shapes Nature creates are among the most beautiful: *"... for I was seeing in a sacred manner the shapes of all things in the spirit, and the shape of all shapes as they must live together like one being."* (BLACK ELK, LAKOTA)

Early in our woodworking ventures Peter and I afforded not one but two rulers and a used Shopsmith Mark V, but no band saw. Furniture refinishing was our gig — reducing, reusing and recycling wood. So woodcrafts and custom furniture projects played second saw for a while. But even as the refinishing business flourished in its first year, we lost the will to expand it. There was an unhealthy lack of viable alternatives to caustic stripping chemicals and finishes in use at that time that deflected our aim to live a healthier, environmentally friendly lifestyle. Consequently, we finished refinishing without regret. *"In our every deliberation, we must consider the impact of our decisions on the next seven generations."* (IROQUOIS CONFEDERACY MAXIM)

Temporarily we worked full time jobs while expanding our woodworking skills in our hobby hours, reassessing how to integrate our self-employment objective with our woodworking interests and respect for Nature.

Suddenly, commercial eco-friendly finishes emerged. Great news! With that we decided we'd resume independence as eco-friendly designer/woodcrafters.

I hoped to soon afford a band saw and scroll saw to recreate Nature's shapes I was drawn to all my life. But my first pick was a hiking sidekick — a serviceable photography outfit for exploring all those natural shapes. *"Listen to all the teachers in the woods. Watch the trees, the animals and all living things — you'll learn more from them than from books."* (JOE COYHIS, MOHICAN) Nature communing was my unequivocal all-time passion and artistic inspiration, also indulging the ardent adventurer at my core. Reverence for Earth and zeal for natural history was (and still is) my driving force.

Finally, we got our first band saw in 1992, and I went digging for a little book about band saw boxes I had bought years before. I'd been waiting years to explore these boundless boxes. I had studied the author's techniques when I first got the book, and had drawn up several of my own patterns. I found my patterns, but the book had disappeared! It had gotten lost somewhere in the chaos of our busy lives. It had been so long I couldn't remember the title or author's name, nor find the time to shop for a replacement. But I still had the techniques and a general picture of some of the projects in my head. And of course a stack of my own designs I had doodled over the years.

So, when we founded our new woodcrafting business that year, shaping band saw boxes in Nature's image naturally became my woodworking passion. Shapes ruled, and I permanently lost that second ruler!

And that's *really* how I started sculpting band saw boxes.

Epilogue…

Ironically, sometime after I began working on this book, I was rummaging through some old storage boxes in the workshop attic looking for stuff for an unrelated project. At the very bottom of a dusty old box of clock parts, lo and behold! *Making Wood Boxes With A Band Saw*, by Tom Crabb! I thumbed through the pages, smiling at the whimsical boxes that presented the basic techniques for my own box designs nearly twenty years earlier. So, over late, I thank my mystery band saw box book writer, Tom Crabb, for providing the structural basis on which all these boxes are built. LKV

comet

Some thought comets were a curse; others believed comets carried angels through the heavens. But modern woodworkers recently discovered the truth: the Comet is just a box made out of wood! Light sapwood on this walnut box together with its maple drawer pull highlight the motion of this frosty Comet streaking through the darkness of space.

surf

These little single-drawer boxes are just as appealing as larger box sculptures. They can also be enlarged a little in height and width, allowing you to cut two sections in the drawer. This Surf reminds me of one of those big waves that comes along that's too risky to body surf — you take that last minute plunge into the curl to avoid its hammering break from nailing you into the ocean floor!

leaf

Nature displays her grandeur in the smallest of her creations. Snowflakes tend to grab the glory for uniqueness, but I've never seen two leaves exactly alike. Each one is its own work of art, whether still attached to twig or fluttering to the ground, like this one.

minnow

Myriads of metallic minnows magically flit through the shallows of my favorite mountain ponds and streams. Light sapwood on dark walnut flashes like bright sunlight on tiny iridescent bodies through dark ripples.

whale play

Gray whales are often seen playing off the shores of the U.S. Pacific coast. If you select a board with contrasting sapwood along at least one edge, you can create the illusion of your top "whale" breaking the sea's surface in a froth of white foam.

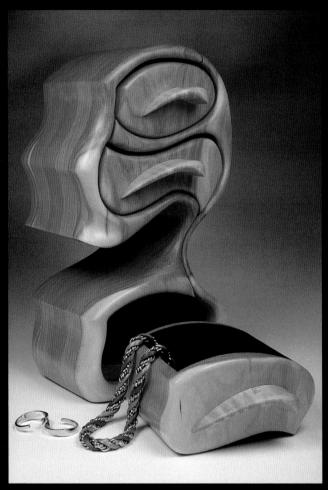

wind tree

A symbol of strength and flexibility. A tree-bute to the woodworker's hardy best friend, and to the flexibility of sculpting band saw boxes. Try a taller variation, or a many-branched version.

little rock

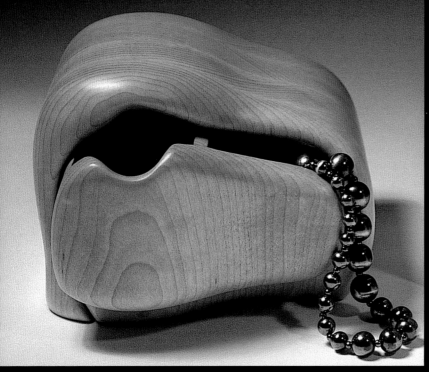

Look closely: on the shores of brooks and streams, you can pick out the distinct features of each smooth, rounded river stone. This Little Rock with a curved front in rock maple has a kidney bean-shaped front just like the top, and can hold your favorite polished pebble collection. Practice the technique of cutting a gentle wave across your box front before cutting out the drawer. Your little sculptures will take on additional dimension! (Save the cutoff from the box front. Temporarily taping it back on gives you a flat surface for clamping parts back together.)

twister 2

"Tornado Alley" — loved and hated at Pittsburgh, PA's annual Three Rivers Arts Festival. It's the hottest outdoor spot for artists to market their wares on sunny June days. But spring storms race up the Ohio River. Winds intensify. They funnel through tall buildings, smack into Gateway Tower #3, whirl around the Pittsburgh Hilton. In seconds, some artists' booths twist into tattered debris. Others remain untouched. After that, salvageable art could fit into this box!

cobra and boa

To the ancient Egyptians, the snake symbolized the beginning and the end of time. I'm always awe-struck when I spot a six-foot long black snake, still as stone, clinging to the side of a tree like a thick meandering fire hose imitating a vine. Solid as the wood to which it's attached, it defies gravity with its sinewy strength. These snakes are gentle and beneficial giants here in the Appalachians. And these boxes are fun and easy to add your own variations, with or without finger slots. Or try out some thin vertical drawer pulls to resemble the pupil slits in a snake's eyes.

pisces

The Fishes. The twelfth sign of the zodiac. The splash of colors and pattern in this poplar Pisces is a dazzling example of bookmatch lamination "special effects."

anniversary box

"A love so true it shines like gold." This walnut box with shining golden birdseye maple laminated to the drawer fronts is a one-of-a-kind created for a special couple. But that doesn't mean you can't make one for a business' establishment anniversary, your sister's birthday or your own in-laws' anniversary.

rock box

This double-entendre box can be seen as a boulder encasing your big diamonds or simply a holder for a collection of your favorite found "lucky stones." The drawer pulls can represent all those one-of-a-kind pebbles you find awash on the shores and in the shallows of a rushing mountain stream. The box body itself is modeled after the big boulders mid-stream that offer themselves up as relaxing retreats for weary woodworkers.

undertow

This wavy box with deep drawers is meant to fill that niche of small, low shelves and other shallow places. My dad's Undertow gushes with gift golf tees as abundant as grains of sand at the bottom of the ocean!

tsunami

Ancient Japanese coastal monuments warn of these huge, geologically induced tidal swells. This is one of my favorite designs. I've made four different sizes: a 12" (photo at right), a 14" with four-drawers (bottom right), a 10" × 5" with two drawers (photo above) and a 9" × 4" with a single drawer (page 114). The bubbling birdseye maple Tsunami remains one of my all-time favorite box sculptures.

cetacean migration

Many species of whales and dolphins travel north in summer to feed and south in winter to breed. The drawers and pulls of this box embody the diversity of migrating whale and porpoise species. But the outer box shape unmistakably resembles the magnificent blue whale, possibly the largest creature ever to live on Earth.

the tides

Earth's waters sway to ancient rhythms of the cosmos. Small box, big statement. Light maple drawer pulls against dark walnut enhance the ebb and flow of this box.

airborne

(Setting a small thought free gives it the chance to become *Airborne*. A soaring turkey vulture with its fingered wingtips modeled for this box. The buzzard is a homely, gangly creature on the ground, but once it is airborne its ability to rise on mountain thermals and soar with peaceful grace is the envy of anyone who can only imagine such freedom. Reversed, this box is the left half of phoenix.)

phoenix

Reborn from its own ash, the Phoenix heralds renewal and the dawn of a new age. Phoenix arose as a variation on the Airborne box. This walnut-and-birds-eye box with its 20"-plus wingspan rises only 6½" but certainly creates a presence, casting a 32" walnut avian shadow base in a duel reflection from above.

(LEFT TO RIGHT)

minnow, surf and biped 1

Enchanting underwater seascapes you see in deep-sea documentaries supply a wealth of wondrous subjects to render in wood. Better yet, put on a mask, snorkel and some flippers and take a swim around your friendly neighborhood coral reef! (Don't we all wish we could do that after a hard day of hand sanding?) Biped — many inquisitive naturalists speculate as to what the first two-legged creatures may have looked like. Dinosaurs, birds, hominids — put them all together and you have this funky box. You can add drawer pulls, finger slots, or just slide the drawers open from their back edges.

peace dove

Send a fellow wood-worker an olive branch. (Maybe he'll make a band saw box out of it!)

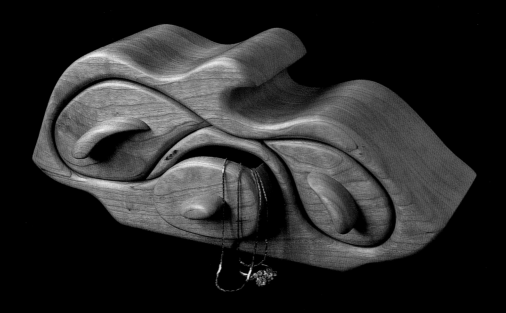

aurora

Goddess of the Dawn. Solar winds ruffle luminous curtains of magnetic activity in Earth's ionosphere. A typically uninteresting wood, this piece of poplar (photo at left) materialized into the most stunning Aurora. Varying shades of moss and emerald greens, pale pinks to blackish-purples, golden yellows and creams — one of the prettiest pieces of wood I can remember. These cherry and walnut Aurora's have their own unique appeal too.

germinating box

New growth teaches us to reach for the sky. A piece of walnut with contrasting maple drawer pulls grew into a handsome three-drawer Germinating Box. Below, a gorgeous piece of poplar with olive and moss colored streaks through the heart of its creamy flesh make this box really look like the time-lapse progression of a young seed breaking out of its coat on a mossy, damp forest floor, reaching for light.

contemporary bowed-side box

"And now for something completely different." When designer's block strikes you, watch a marathon of Monty Python's Flying Circus episodes. Guaranteed to make you a silly person. Monty Python has their version of "Spamalot," but I wanted to make a band saw box I didn't have to "Sandalot." What a silly woodworking concept! (Every woodworker likes to sand a lot, don't they?)

ophidian

Any member of the suborder Ophidia: The Serpents. This cherry box is a depiction of seething nests of timber rattlers and copperheads in my region that become active when spring warms their rocky reptilian dens. Carving can be a challenge on the end grain of harder woods when making this box. Sharp chisels are a must!

lotus

Flower of the Pure Land. This box sprouted from one 12" and another 14" Germinating Box. I managed to find two very long, very chocolaty walnut boards cut consecutively from the same tree. As I planed them, a rainbow of mocha, red and dark golden brown colors melted throughout the grain of each board. Mmm! Pure paradise for any woodworker!

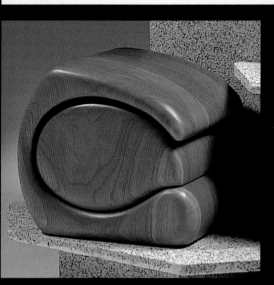

seed, pod

The naturalist in me can become absorbed in observing plants in various stages of growth and reproduction. I think of these two little boxes as time-lapse photographs — the seed developing within the Pod, and later the Seed beginning to punch its first root through its coat.

Sun embraces fertile Earth on the Wheel of the Year, as new life springs forth amid life-giving rains. I struck woodworker's gold when I found several long, rough-cut boards of worm-streaked maple buried in the back shed of a small sawmill. A walnut base and branching tree complement soft olives and browns drizzling down this maple sculpture. When I first cut the outer box shapes, to my delight, in the bookmatched laminations of the left box top I came face-to-face with a cleverly hidden forest fox!

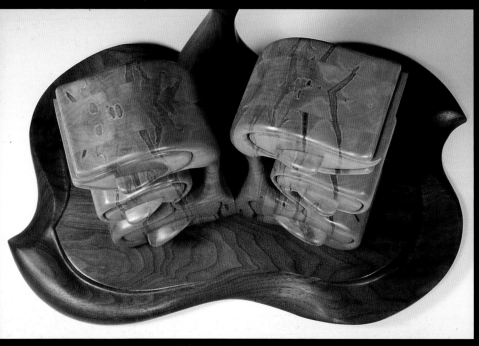

shroom

A real fun guy. Mycological subjects are one of my favorites to photograph when wandering the temperate Appalachian rainforests. Such colorful and interesting varieties in the fungus family! A fellow box maker gave me this solid block of western willow. It looked rather uninteresting and sat in my shop for at least a year. But when I finally cut and carved some sweeping curves, what a stunning swirl of grain did I find inside!

patterns

The Shapes of Things to Come For your sculpting pleasure, the following pages contain twenty patterns for you to shape into a diversity of drawered
boxes. You can use them to hone techniques demonstrated in the previous
chapters, modify them to suit your individual taste, or simply draw upon them
as inspiration for your own functional organic creations.

These designs have been popular among art collectors, art and craft show
patrons, gallery proprietors, craftsman's guilds, art juries and, most important
of all, family members and friends. Most of the containers contained here were
drafted with ease of sanding in mind, so curves are broad, easy to machine sand
and can be shaped with a minimum of tools and tool accessory sizes. But there's
no reason why you can't sharpen some of the curves and morph any of the designs into something even more wild and wavy. That's the fun of sculpting band
saw boxes!

The patterns include enlargement percentages for those boxes too big to fit
on the pages of this book. (The grid lines on each pattern represent 1" squares
when scaled to size.) Some patterns will require $8^1/_2 \times 14$ paper when enlarged.
Or you can just do the handyman woodworker version and make two, $8^1/_2 \times 11$
copies, piecing the pages together with clear tape. On some of the patterns you
will notice details, options or carving suggestions particular to that design.

The solid lines of each pattern represent lines you will cut with your band
saw, such as the outer box shape and drawers. Solid lines also represent the patterns for drawer pulls. (Cut pulls out of a separate piece of scrap wood, not out
of the drawer fronts!) The dotted lines indicate where you will cut out the inner
sections of the drawers, pieces of the backs of certain boxes, and carving suggestions on the box fronts. Don't forget, you can mirror most of the carving suggestions for the box fronts on the backs of your boxes too, giving your entire box
sculpture more depth and variety of shape overall. Just make sure you don't get
a little overzealous with your back carving. You may end up carving a hole right
through the back of the box and into the hollow part! Well, the exception is the
holes drilled in the back of the Anniversary Box — they are meant to be there,
as you will see.

The fun is just beginning...LKV

comet

(page 88)

For full-size pattern enlarge 122%.

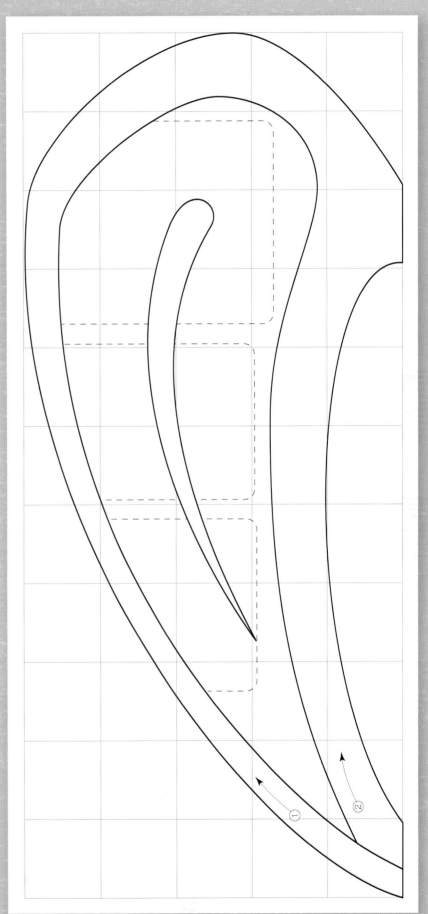

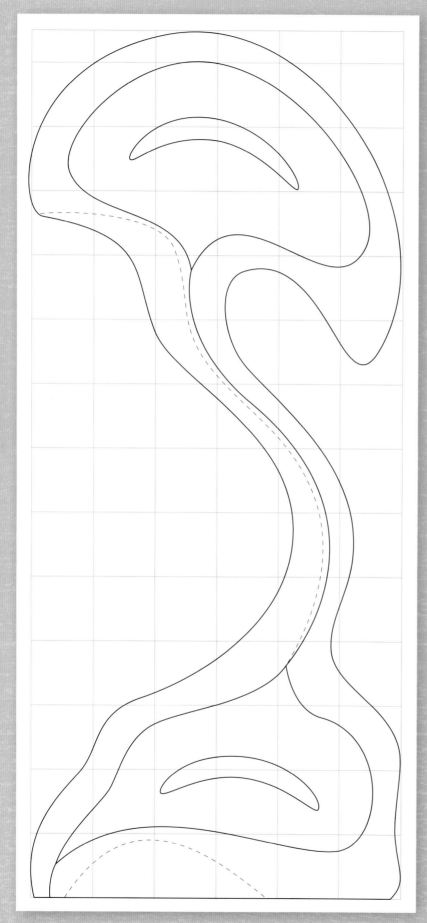

shroom

(page 105)

For full-size pattern enlarge149%.

ophidian
(page 102)

For full-size pattern
enlarge 122% .

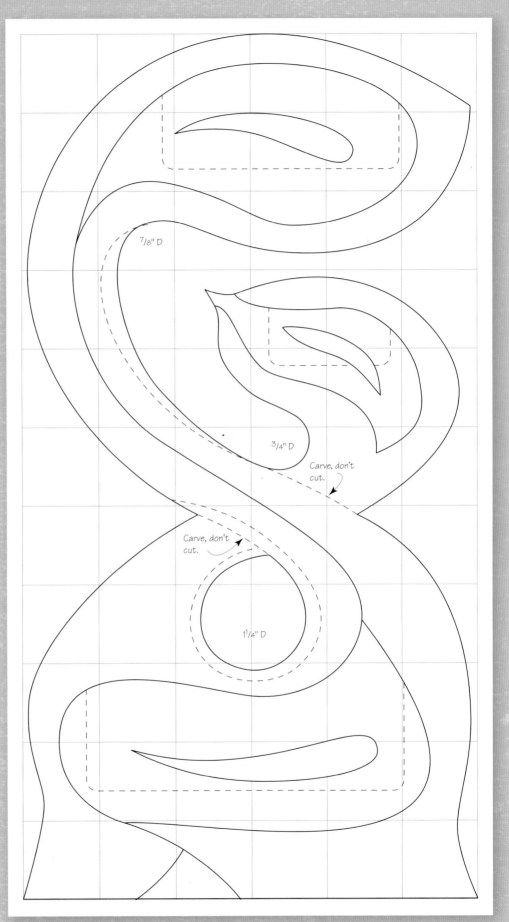

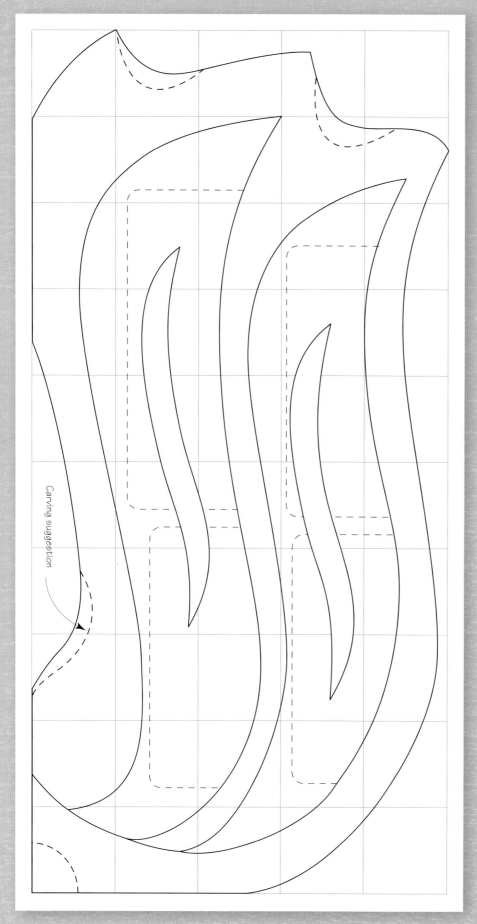

Carving suggestion

phoenix 1 (a.k.a. airborne)

(page 98)

For full-size pattern
enlarge 111%.

For full-size pattern enlarge 111%.

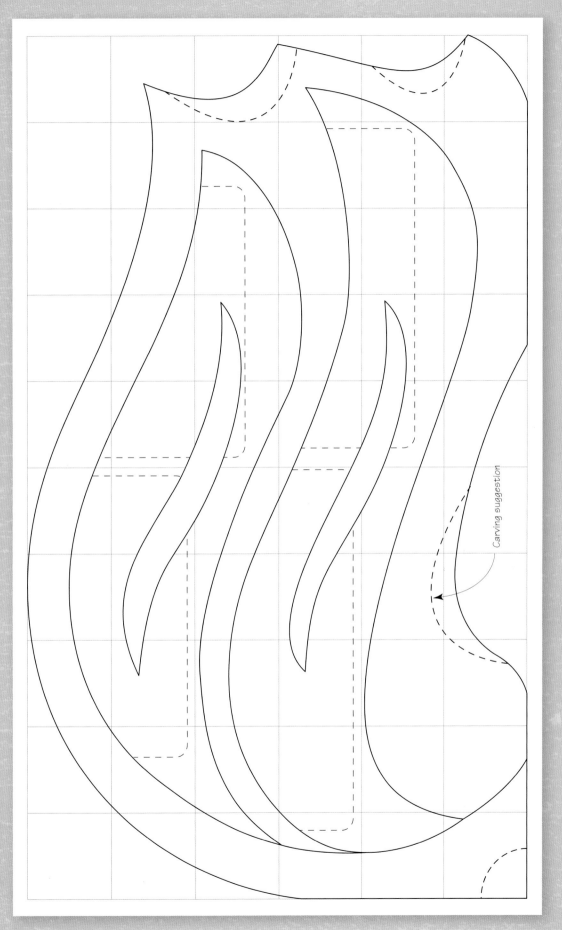

Carving suggestion

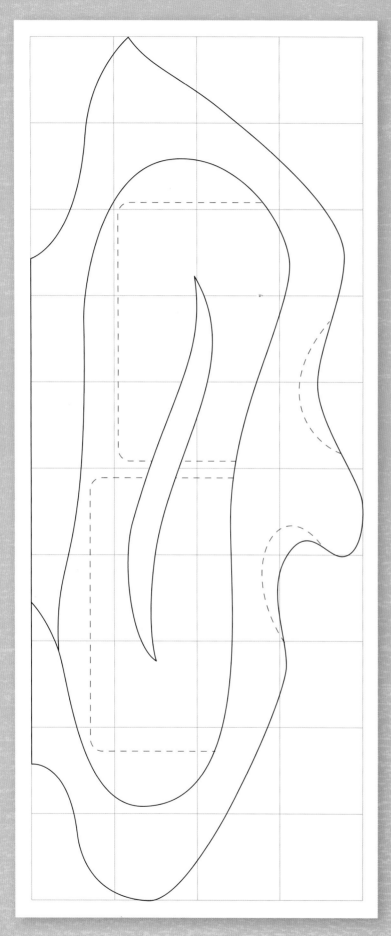

little peace dove

For full-size pattern enlarge 111%.

peace dove
(page 99)

For full-size pattern enlarge 145%.

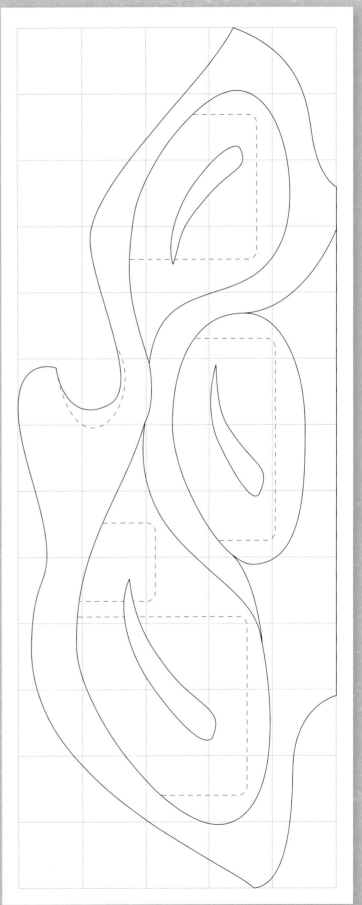

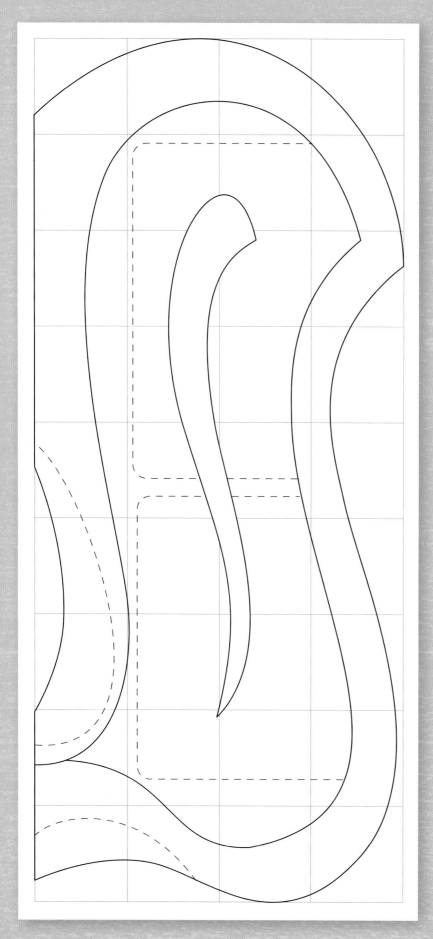

tsunami 1-drawer

(Photo is 2-drawer version.)

Pattern shown full size.

anniversary
(page 93)

For full-size pattern
enlarge 122%.

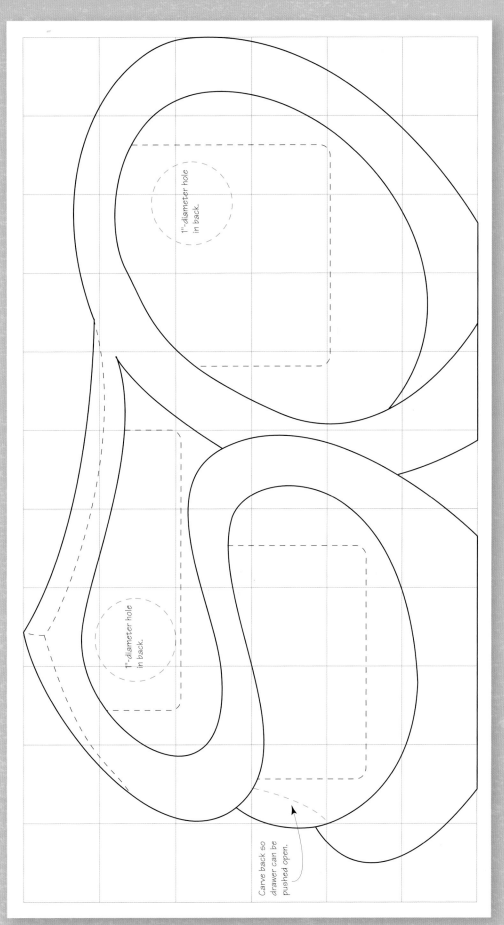

1"-diameter hole
in back.

1"-diameter hole
in back.

Carve back so
drawer can be
pushed open.

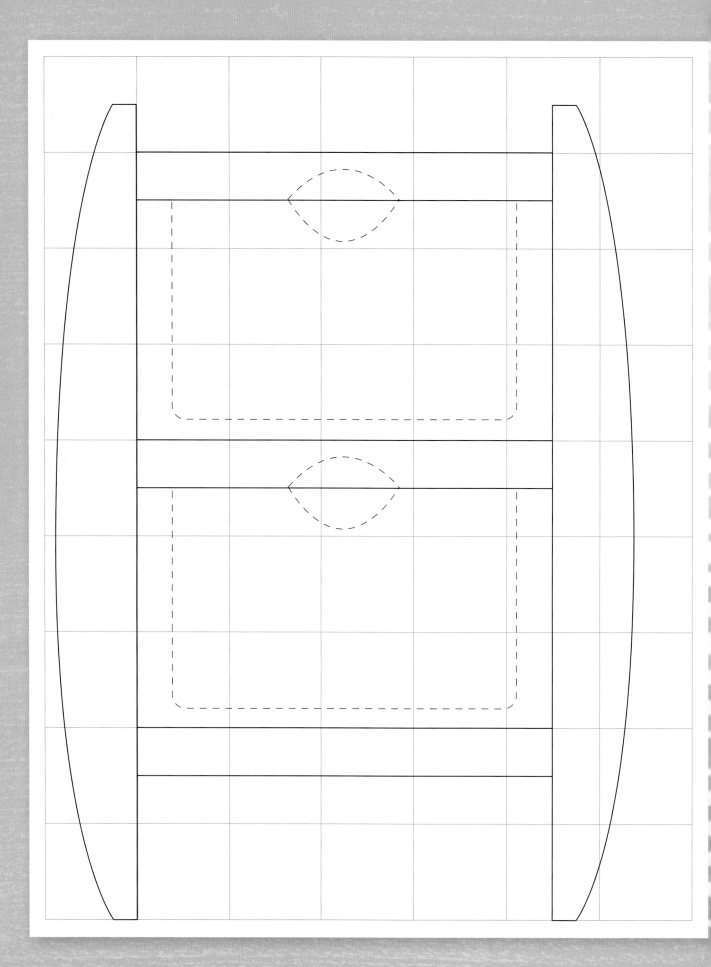

contemporary 2-drawer
(page 102)

Pattern shown full size.

undertow
(page 94)

For full-size pattern enlarge 156%.

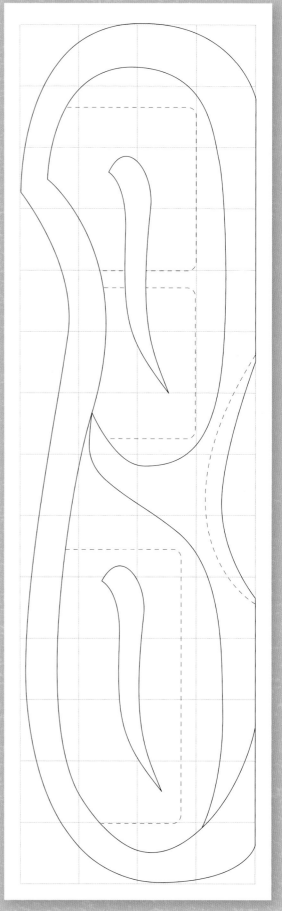

biped-1

(page 99)

Pattern shown full size.

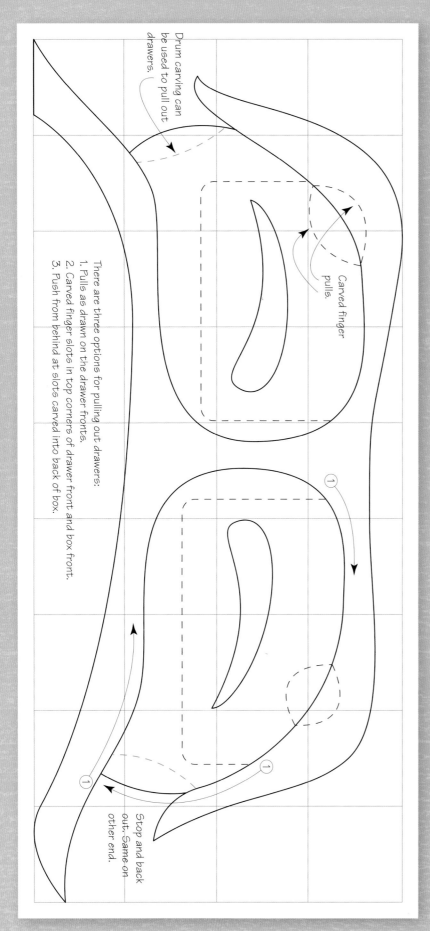

Drum carving can be used to pull out drawers.

Carved finger pulls.

There are three options for pulling out drawers:
1. Pulls as drawn on the drawer fronts.
2. Carved finger slots in top corners of drawer front and box front.
3. Push from behind at slots carved into back of box.

Stop and back out. Same on other end.

1

1

1

118

biped-2

For full-size pattern enlarge 112%.

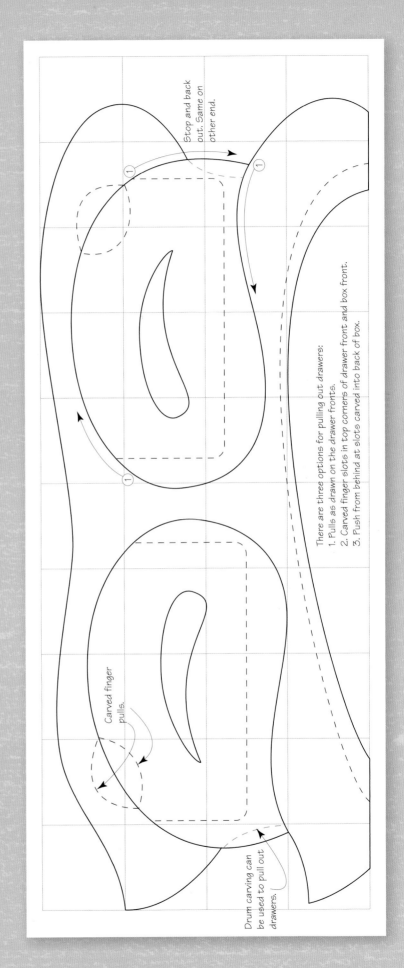

Stop and back out. Same on other end.

There are three options for pulling out drawers:
1. Pulls as drawn on the drawer fronts.
2. Carved finger slots in top corners of drawer front and box front.
3. Push from behind at slots carved into back of box.

Carved finger pulls.

Drum carving can be used to pull out drawers.

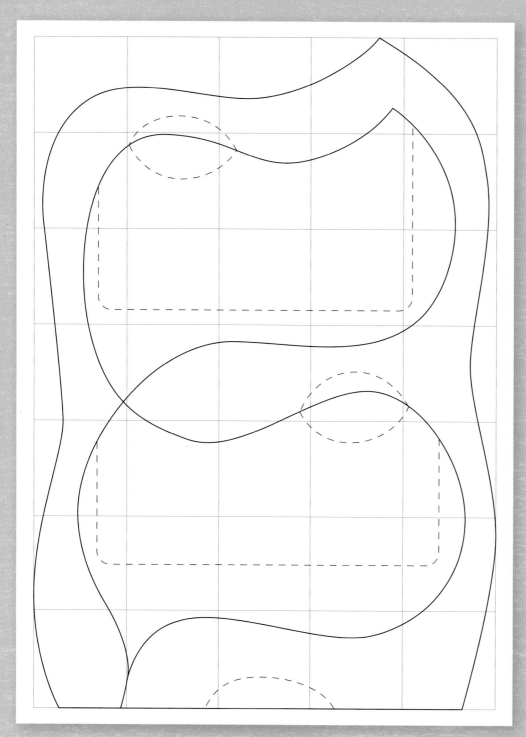

twister-2
(page 91)

Pattern shown full size.

twister-3

Pattern shown full size.

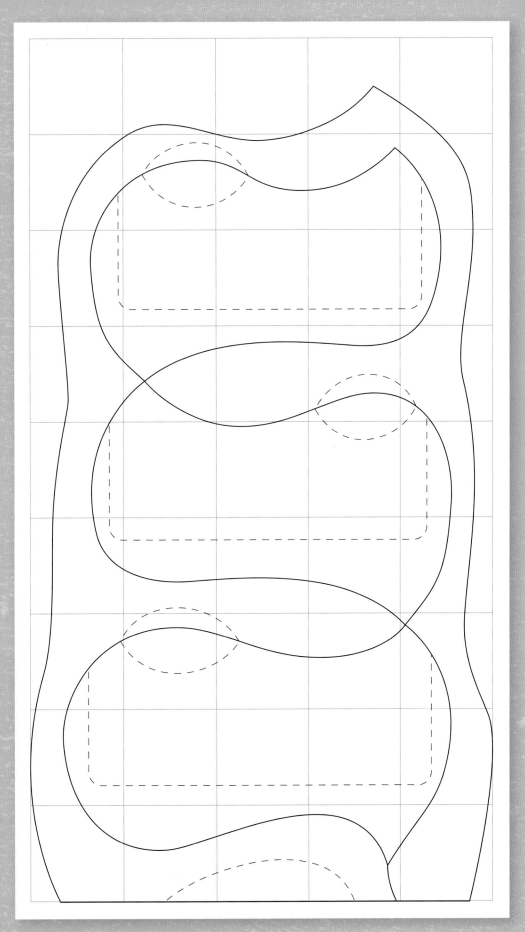

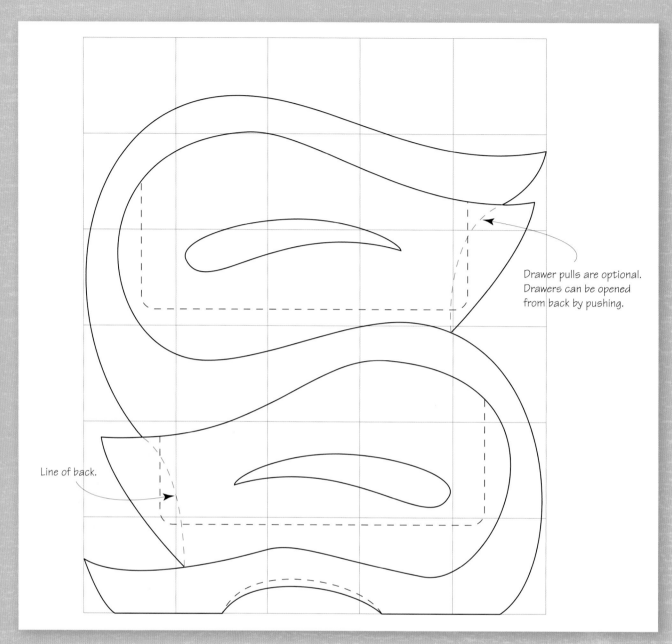

Drawer pulls are optional.
Drawers can be opened
from back by pushing.

Line of back.

aurora-2

Pattern shown full size.

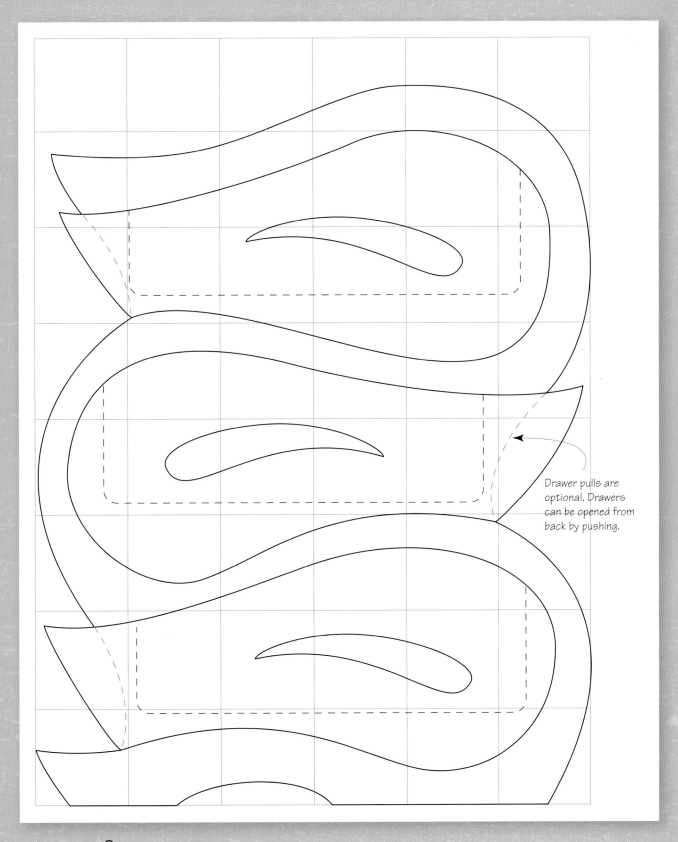

Drawer pulls are optional. Drawers can be opened from back by pushing.

aurora-3

Pattern shown full size.

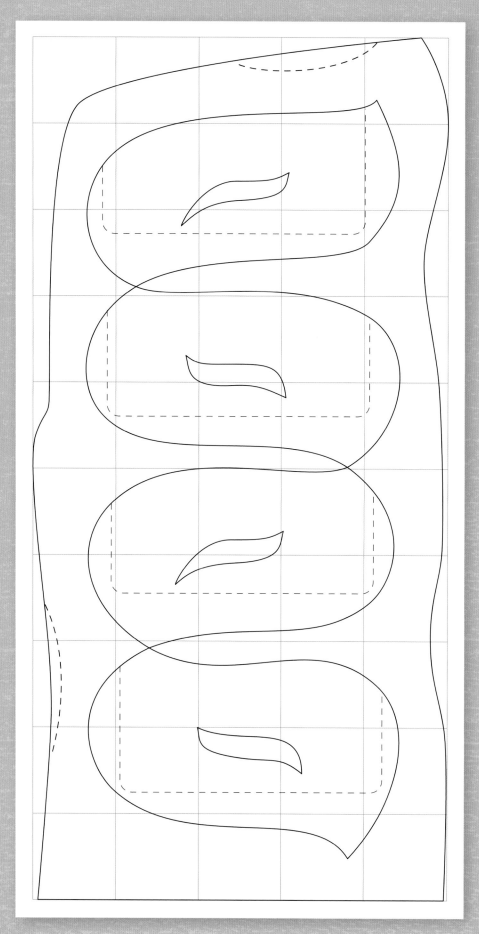

forest stump
"life is like a
box..."

For full-size pattern
enlarge 111%.

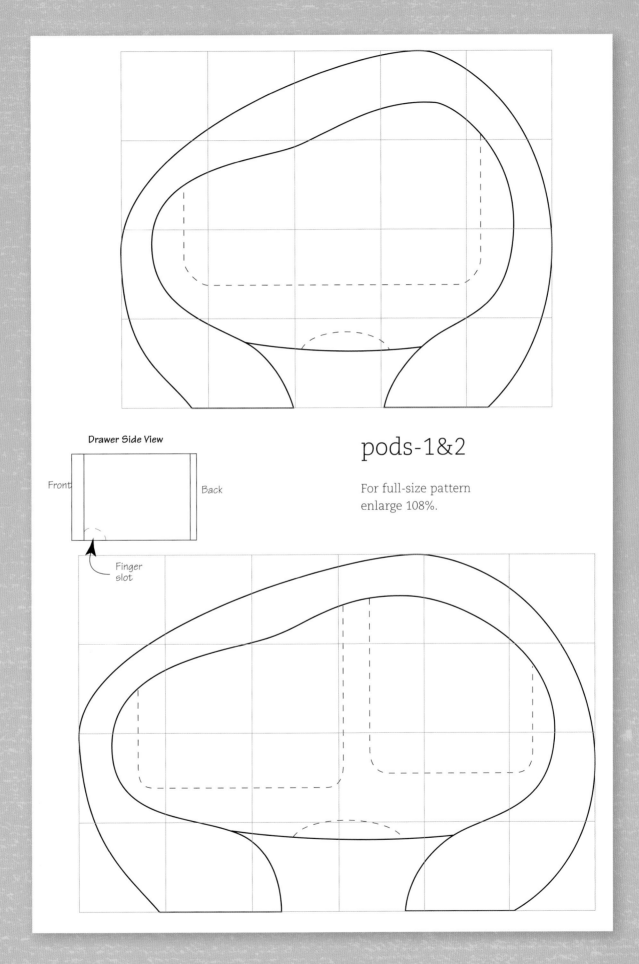

Drawer Side View

Front

Back

Finger
slot

pods-1&2

For full-size pattern
enlarge 108%.

suppliers

AIRWARE AMERICA
800-328-1792
www.airwareamerica.com
Airmate HEPA filter systems and headpieces. A must for dust!

BAND SAW BLADES, INC.
800-342-9625
www.bandsawblades.com
Band saw blades

BOISHIELD PAINT CO.
800-621-2591
www.bioshieldpaint.com
Bio-friendly oil finishes and thinners

CARTER
888.622.7837
www.carterproducts.com
band saw products, parts and supplies

COLUMBIA FOREST PRODUCTS
www.columbiaforestproducts.com
Wood, hardware, tools, books

CONSTANTINE'S WOOD CENTER OF FLORIDA
800-443-9667
www.constantines.com
Tools, woods, veneers, hardware, finishing supplies

DREMEL
800-437-3635
www.dremel.com
Rotary tools, drivers, scroll saws, glue guns

DONJER PRODUCTS CORP
800-336-6537
www.donjer.com
Suede Tex flocking

FRANK PAXTON LUMBER COMPANY
www.paxtonwood.com
Wood, tools, books

THE HOME DEPOT
800-430-3376 (U.S.)
800-628-0525 (Canada)
www.homedepot.com
Woodworking tools, supplies and hardware

HOBBY & CRAFT FLOCKING FIBERS AND FLOCKING SUPPLIES
www.craftflocking.com
Flocking supplies

KLINGSPOR ABRASIVES INC.
800-645-5555
www.klingspor.com
Sandpaper of all kinds

LOWE'S COMPANIES, INC.
800-445-6937
www.lowes.com
Woodworking tools, supplies and hardware

PORTER CABLE
www.deltaportercable.com
Woodworking power tools

ROCKLER WOODWORKING AND HARDWARE
800-279-4441
www.rockler.com
Woodworking tools, hardware, flocking supplies and books

ROSEBURG FOREST PRODUCTS
800-245-1115
www.rfpco.com
Wood, hardware, tools, books

ROTO-ZIP
877-768-6947
www.rotozip.com
Hand-held power cutting and carving tools

SAWS UK
www.sawsuk.com
Saw blades, band saw blades

SUPER CUTS
www.supercutsblade.com.au
Saw blades, band saw blades

USA LIVOS DISTRIBUTOR
503-257-9663
www.livos.us
Oil finishes, thinners and waxes. The trendsetter in environmentally friendly and hypoallergenic finishes.

WOODCRAFT BANDS, INC.
800-582-1328
www.woodcraftbands.com
Band saw blades

WOODCRAFT SUPPLY LLC
800-225-1153
www.woodcraft.com
Woodworking tools, hardware, flocking supplies and books

WOODWORKER'S HARDWARE
800-383-0130
www.wwhardware.com
Woodworking hardware

WOODWORKER'S SUPPLY
800-645-9292
http://woodworker.com
Woodworking tools and accessories, finishing supplies, books and plans

index

More great titles from Popular Woodworking!

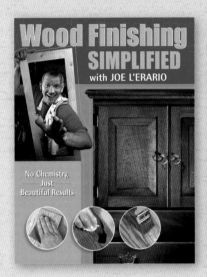
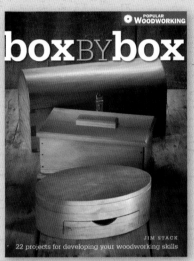

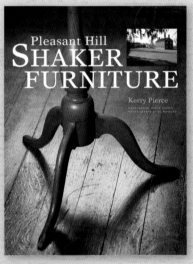